P9-CPY-362

THIS IS *NOT* A FASHION STORY

THIS IS *NOT* A FASHION STORY

DANIELLE BERNSTEIN
WITH EMILY SIEGEL

2681 Spruill Avenue
North Charleston, SC 29405
Vertel is a registered trademark of Nextone Inc.
Visit our website at www.vertelpublishing.com.

© 2020 by Danielle Bernstein

All rights reserved. This book or any portion thereof may not be reproduced or used in any
manner whatsoever without the express written permission of the publisher except for the use of
brief quotations in a book review.

First Edition

Library of Congress Control Number: 2020901973

ISBN-13: 978-1-64112-017-3
ISBN-10: 1-64112-017-7

eBook ISBN: 9781641129428

This book depicts events in the author's life as accurately as present recollection permits. Some names and identifying characteristics have been changed to respect the privacy of certain individuals. Some dialogue has been re-created.

Dedicated to Poppy Ivan, who always believed fashion was more than a shopping habit. And to Poppy Dave, who threatened to break my boyfriends' legs if they hurt me.

Contents

Let's Rewind

Five years ago, on the kind of bright morning that reminds me why I want to live in Manhattan, I woke up beside a naked male model and decided to write a book.

His name was Elevator Hunk. Obviously that's not the guy's legal name—his passport doesn't list "Elevator Hunk" above his birthdate—but it *was* the nickname my friends and I gave him during our many weeks of stalking. You see, Elevator Hunk and I happened to live in the same apartment building in the West Village of Manhattan. He was the first thing I had noticed about my new digs, aside from the luxury of *finally* having an in-unit laundry machine (the pinnacle of New York living).

The timing was fortuitous, because I moved into this particular apartment during the May of 2015—at a time when I was recovering from a bad breakup and had decided to let myself enjoy the joys of sex without commitment. I like to call those months my "Samantha Summer," so named after Kim Cattrall's legendary character on *Sex and the City*. Samantha Jones lived and loved freely. She got what she wanted. And what's more, she refused to apologize for wanting it.

But back to that Saturday morning. I watched Elevator Hunk's ass slip out of my cotton jersey sheets looking like two scoops of salted caramel ice cream…then swiped my phone off the bedside table. One extremely long text to my girls later, I detailed exactly how he got there. (Don't worry; you'll read about it later.) My phone started pinging incessantly, receiving a gaggle of hilarious responses. The most popular opinion? That I would want to remember this movielike experience when I was old and married. A memorializing text simply wasn't enough.

Then I started to think. Why not put pen to paper and write about *all* the wild encounters from my Samantha Summer? Most likely no one else would want to read it, but I'd at least have the memories.

Lucky—or perhaps unlucky—for me, I had a six-hour flight to Los Angeles that very day. Once the plane took off, I applied my Dr. Jart+ sheet mask, grabbed my laptop, and started to chronicle. Every dirty detail.

By the time I returned to New York five days later, I was addicted to writing. I had already transcribed an additional four sex-capades while on the West Coast, stories that detailed the various men and experiences in my twenty-three years of life. I started to think that maybe, just maybe, it could be a book that people would actually want to read. *This* book.

I gave my project a working title—*The Samantha Stories*—and spent every spare moment of the next weeks hammering on my keyboard. Of course, I am used to sharing the particulars of my life on *WeWoreWhat*, but my sex life…that had always been private. Like many women, I was afraid of being judged for my sexuality. There's a four-letter word wrongly reserved for women so transparent about their desires.

But the more I thought about it, the more I wondered why not bare it all? Why couldn't I be an "influencer" in the larger sense, helping to destigmatize casual sex for a new generation of women? In that way, I could *truly* become Samantha.

So I wrote. And I wrote. Then a few weeks later, I shared the sample chapters with some friends in my inner circle. I was ready to bask in their adulation—to let their compliments wash over me—but they all told me *not* to publish the book. To stop writing immediately.

"You should write about business, not sex," one of them told me over a late-night plate of duck confit at Hudson Clearwater. "If you publish this, everyone is going to think you're a whore. Your family will be ashamed. Advertisers won't want to work with you. The public doesn't need to know that side of you."

Those words really stuck with me. What was so wrong with *that* side of me? The side that could divorce romance from sex? That enabled me to embrace my physical cravings without the confines of a relationship? It seemed as if my sexual liberation, if made public, would label me a slut and potentially even ruin my career.

Only now, years later, do I realize what a load of bullshit this all was. I am not a slut. Never have been, never will be. I am actually a serial monogamist who prefers to be in long-term relationships. It's only in between those boyfriends that I have given myself the freedom to explore casual sex. And what's so bad about that, as long as it's always my choice and I'm cautious and safe?

The answer became clear: if I was going to write a book, then that book would need to share everything. Give my readers more than how-to tips on making it in the fashion industry or becoming a successful social media influencer. I wanted to share the real me, the good and the bad, without fearing that people will forget I am still just twenty-seven years old and therefore prone to making mistakes. Over the past decade as I grew my brand on *WeWoreWhat*, I put myself out there for the world to see. I didn't just grow a business; I grew in life, learning and failing and succeeding in my own way.

Five years ago, I wasn't ready to write that particular book.

But now I am. So let's rewind.

———————

I, Danielle Bernstein, burst into the world sometime around 3:00 a.m. on May 28, 1992. At the time, my mom, dad, and brother were living with my grandparents while saving up for a house. Labor pains jolted my mom awake in her childhood bedroom, and she barely made it to the Long Island Jewish Hospital before I flew out. It's an ongoing joke with my mom that giving birth was the easiest part of raising me.

I grew up in a simpler time: the 1990s. Sure, we had the internet, but it was used for little more than email, Ask Jeeves, and MapQuest. Hell, this was back when Martha Stewart was the world's first and only lifestyle influencer (not that we'd yet created that term).

As a young girl, I was obsessed with clothes. I spent hours on my bedroom floor, cutting pages out of *Vogue* and taping collages to my walls. The only thing I loved more than fashion magazines was putting looks together. By the time I entered the sixth grade, I needed to change my outfit fifty times before I was ready for school. (I was really good at ignoring my mother's screams to "get my ass in the car.") I think it actually took me longer to get ready for a day of middle school than it does now.

Everyone else already seemed to know where I was headed. (Just watch the VHS recording of my bat mitzvah, which is full of my friends professing that I was destined for a future in fashion.) I, however, had yet to dream about a career in fashion. I just figured that, like most girls, I really liked shopping.

Back then, my only goal was to eventually live in Manhattan. To be one of the glamorous people living in that glamorous place. I taught myself how to binge-watch *Sex and the City* while my mom was out of the house. (Andrea Bernstein loves *SatC* as much as the next person, but felt I was too young to watch at the time.) However, I was in love with the Fab Four's magical world, and nothing was going to stop me from tuning in.

To me, every episode of that show was like a perfect, thirty-minute, all-expenses-paid trip to the isle of Manhattan—a mythical place where all a girl needs is her career, her friends, and a killer pair of Manolo Blahniks. In New York, any*one* could be any*thing*...so long as they had the outfit and confidence to match.

Unfortunately, Glenn and Andrea Bernstein had chosen to leave Manhattan for the Long Island suburbs after my brothers and I were born. Jack, Alec, and I grew up in Great Neck, a picturesque town best known for its short commute to New York City and representation in *The Great Gatsby*. But despite its close proximity, Manhattan may as well have been on a different planet. We Bernsteins rarely ventured into "the city." The creature comforts of our community were simply too enticing, too comfortable, to pass up. Why visit the Big Apple when the Roosevelt Field Mall was just ten minutes away?

Perhaps that suburban monotony is why I became so obsessed with my future self. I would dream about that day I'd move to Manhattan and rent a cute West Village studio. I would fill the space with Restoration Hardware furniture, date handsome investment bankers, and shop at the most exclusive stores on Fifth Avenue. (Somehow, even as a tween, I had already developed quite expensive tastes.)

Then my twelfth birthday rolled around. Having zero concept of real estate prices, I asked my parents for an apartment in New York City. (Oh, how they must have laughed when I unwrapped that Polly Pocket.) I was a kid, but I was growing impatient with my youth. I had already started to feel like childhood was something I *just had to get through* before my real life could begin.

Years later, at the tender age of nineteen, I finally moved to New York. I found an apartment in Greenwich Village, but this was not the adorable studio of my dreams. For years, I lived in a cramped one bedroom with not one, but *three* other girls (and a window unit precarious enough to threaten anyone who walked beneath it). But I didn't care. That apartment might as well have been the penthouse at the Pierre. All that mattered was that I finally had a Manhattan address.

My first years in the city were anything but chic. I spent more time shopping in bodegas than Balenciaga, more time riding the A train than in black cars. Most newcomers find New York overwhelming, and I was no exception. The noise, the chaos, the filth… this was nothing like the New York of my dreams. I quickly learned to love my city and all its flaws, but initially it was a shock to the senses. I spent those first months with a train ticket always in my purse, ready to flee the Big Bad City for the safety of my mother. (What can I say? The woman makes a mean lasagna.)

All this to say, my path was not always paved with proverbial roses.

Here's the truth: I founded *WeWoreWhat* shortly after moving to New York with zero thoughts of turning it into a career. I'm more shocked than anyone that my little passion project has grown into a multimillion-dollar business. The blog started as a hobby—something fun to help me carve my own path in the city while attending fashion school. I had always been the friend girls would text with fashion questions (as my bat mitzvah montage shows), and I eventually figured: Why not put my sage wisdom online? And if it helped my readers get dressed with a little more confidence…then all the better.

I've worked my Pilates-toned ass off to launch this business, but there are also many external reasons for *WeWoreWhat*'s success. For one, I was an early adopter of Instagram, the platform that has come to define life as an influencer. I also happened to launch my blog just as print media was on the decline, which sent readers on the hunt for other types of content. For the first time, people were looking beyond the world of traditional publishing. The year 2010 was precisely the perfect time for a budding blogger to enter the digital landscape—a time when readers were open to finding new (and perhaps more relatable voices), but social media had yet to become oversaturated.

Critics like to say that I was in the right place at the right time. And while it's true Lady Luck has been on my side, she's only *part* of the reason why *WeWoreWhat* has prospered. My business succeeded because it's authentic. Because it is me, and I am it. My blog is the digital equivalent of me, a young fashionista with the attitude of an outlaw. But unlike my beloved inspiration, *Sex and the City*, I felt it important that my brand be just as attainable as it was glamorous.

Four boyfriends, seven apartments, and two million Instagram followers later…I'm proud to say that I *finally* have my own place in the West Village. (Unless you count my French bulldogs, Brooklyn and Bleecker, as roommates.) Sometimes my version of Mannhabitation includes star-studded events at Cipriani, and sometimes it includes bingeing *The Bachelor* on my living room floor. While reading this book, I need you to picture the latter—to pretend that we're at home on my cozy Timothy Oulton couch, eating Hu chocolate and Skinny Pop popcorn, gabbing in sweatpants while I beg my dog to stop humping your arm. (Like mother, like son, I suppose.)

This book tells the story of a girl who grew up yearning for her spot at the grown-up table. Of a teenager who dreamed of working at the highest levels of the fashion industry. Of a young woman who dated every kind of guy New York has to offer. Of an established influencer sitting front row at Tom Ford before she could legally order her own cocktails (tequila on the rocks, please!). Of a CEO signing seven-figure deals and launching a tech company before her thirtieth birthday.

Of course, there were stumbles along the way. I worked hard to get where I am and am not embarrassed to say that I've had to learn from my many mistakes..

There was that time I lost hundreds of thousands of dollars on a failed shoe brand. The two times I let a man threaten my self-worth. I promise not to sugarcoat things—to say *exactly* how this all happened for me, the good and the bad. The down and dirty of it all. (And yes, I completely expect to equally be criticized and adored for what I put out there in this book.) If I do this right, I can show my readers how to turn their fantasies into realities while having fun along the way. Each "lesson" in this book is told through funny/sad/inspiring anecdotes taken from my life, an amalgamation of my twenty-seven years on this planet. (Which, yes, I realize isn't the *longest* amount of time. But I've managed to pack in a lot.)

This is not a fashion story, but it's not *not* a fashion story. It's just the story of a young woman who shed her suburban roots to forge her own path in the concrete jungle of New York City. It's *my* story. And I'm telling it my way.

LESSON ONE

Keep Calm and Carry On

My Instagram followers know that I'm Jew-*ish*. I'm not a particularly religious person, but I do love the history and sense of community. I also happened to grow up in a town that was 102 percent Jewish, meaning you couldn't throw a TCBY ice cream cone without hitting someone whose last name was Goldstein, Feldstein, or Rosenfeld. So I guess one could say it's a huge part of who I am.

Those of you who aren't East Coast Jews need to know how much we freaking love sleepaway camp. Every summer, the preteen populations of Westchester and Long Island trade suburbia for eight-week stints in greener pork-free pastures. Campers hail from elite towns, love to brag about their parents' careers, and play Jewish Geography like it's their job. (Yes, I do know the

Rosenblums from Scarsdale who own Universal Studios and have a waterfront house on Nantucket.) Jewish summer camps are like a preteen version of the Hamptons, except everyone has braces and no one throws up at the Clam Bar. Not that I would know what that feels like.

Mine was Camp Birchmont in Wolfeboro, New Hampshire. The institution, so named for the abundance of birch trees on its premises, prides itself on being a home away from home. This is a place where cabin chores are used to teach campers responsibility and where the towering White Mountains are always in view. I attended Camp Birchmont for nine consecutive summers, spending eight weeks at the campground every year after the age of eight. My parents *claimed* they were sending us away so that my brothers and I could learn how to be self-sufficient, but I'm pretty sure they just needed a break from us kids. (And who could blame them? We were chaos on wheels.)

I could write an entire book about how much Camp Birchmont means to my family. It's still such a meaningful place that my older brother, Jack, proposed to his fiancée there last summer. Camp was truly a second home for the Bernstein children, a place where we could grow and explore beyond the confines of our comfortable suburb. It's where I learned to rig a sailboat, where I had my first kiss, where an older female counselor taught me how to use a tampon. (TMI? If so, you'll probably want to put this book down. I have a notorious lack of filter.)

As a kid, it never felt like summer could start until we were en route to camp. The first thing I did after boarding the Birchmont Bus? Ditch my older brother, Jack, and younger brother, Alec. (Even then, they were great, cool guys. But for some reason, I used to find them intensely embarrassing. Although I'm sure I was more often the one embarrassing them.)

The person I wanted to find was my bunkmate and partner in crime: Ashley.

Ashley's dad grew up with my mother, so the two of us had been best friends since birth—despite Ashley being, in many ways, my polar opposite. She was quiet; I was loud. She was serious; I was insane. She followed the rules; I broke every single one of them. We made the perfect odd pair.

Ashley and I preferred to sit in the back of the bus, where we could play "MASH," which later graduated to "Fuck, Marry, Kill" in our teenage years. Even though I boasted chubby cheeks and chunky glasses throughout my years at Camp Birchmont, I had been born with the innate confidence that followers have come to expect on my blog. I have always had the self-assurance and desire to connect with people—something that has been both a blessing and a burden.

When our games were done, Ashley and I would spend hours deciding which boy I was going to "date" each year. (Which, at this early point in my life, meant little more than sitting next to each other at camp bonfires.) Ashley, of course, had yet to show much of an interest in the opposite sex.

When we pulled into the campgrounds, I was always amazed by how much it resembled a movie. The place was all craft rooms, mess halls, and daisy-filled meadows. I swam in a placid lake and built miniature cabins out of popsicle sticks. The only thing actually distinguishing this camp from the one portrayed in *Dirty Dancing*? That our dance teacher was more Danny DeVito than Patrick Swayze. (And that my solo talent show routine to "Vamos a la Playa" did not inspire the entire room to jump to their feet. Bummer.)

It wasn't until my seventh summer, when I was fourteen, that I decided I was ready for a *real* boyfriend. The kind who would hold my hand and French kiss me behind the outhouses. Lucky for me, I had just the boy in mind: Jake Rosenthal, new kid and official camp heartthrob.

Even then, I was already attracted to tall, dark, and handsome. (My friends like to joke that all my exes look the same.) And while pre-growth-spurt Jake wasn't necessarily tall, he did have a mop of black curls and shorts that hung low enough to give me a glimpse of his Calvins. Basically, he was the hottest thing I'd ever seen.

Jake was what Camp Birchmont called a "halfer," a term created for campers who came for four weeks instead of the full eight. He arrived halfway through July, fresh meat dropped into the market midseason. Forgetting the ridiculous rhinestone-bedazzled braces that I'd forced my orthodontist to apply in May, I made it my mission to seduce him.

"See that guy?" I whispered to Ashley in the mess hall one morning. "He doesn't know what's coming for him."

Ashley looked up just in time to see Jake pile his already heaping plate with too many scrambled eggs. "Him?" I ignored her lack of enthusiasm and prepared for battle.

Turns out, teenage boys aren't all that complicated. It only took one day's worth of lingering eye contact before Jake asked me to sit with him at the next bonfire. (I had also informed *everyone* about my crush, knowing the gossip would get back to him.) Soon, Jake and I were taking solo sunset hikes and sharing a blanket at the lodge during movie nights. Word spread that we were an item. Danielle and Jake. I like to think they called us *Dake*.

Let me just get this out of the way now: Jake and I are no longer together. (I know; sob.) Still, I learned so much from our time together that summer. Jake taught me that I'll never need lip filler if I kiss boys until my pout is swollen, and that hand stuff behind the dining hall is *always* a good idea. In many ways, it was *the* relationship that turned me into a woman. (No offense to my super-awesome, disco-themed bat mitzvah, which, fortunately for you, I was told didn't warrant its own chapter. But it was sick.)

Jake and I tumbled into puppy love. But this level of pure happiness only made me panic. What would happen to Jake and me after camp? Could our love survive the school year? Or were we destined to become the next Britney and Justin?

Camp Birchmont didn't allow access to computers, so I had to wait until I got home to Google Jake's address. To my delight, I discovered that he lived just fifteen minutes away in a nearby town called Roslyn. Hell, our suburbs even shared a shopping center.

How Jake and I didn't put that together while at camp, I'll never know. What I do know is that the clouds parted and the sun shone through: Jake and I could keep dating at summer's end.

That September, I began my freshman year at Great Neck South High School with an extra boost of confidence. Sure, every girl in my class claimed to have a "camp boyfriend." But mine was real, and I could prove it. He lived just two towns away.

Jake and I managed to keep our relationship going for another year. During the winter, we would alternate weekends between his town and mine. We introduced our friends and threw the best house parties. It was the kind of carefree relationship that you can only have when your biggest concern is whose basement to make out in that evening.

Still, Jake had a lasting impact on who I am today. We went through a lot during our time together. We jointly studied the art of the perfect, over-the-pants movie theater hand job. We also happened to be dating when I found out about my parents' impending divorce. (Although it's difficult to say which experience had a larger impact on who I am today.)

I'll dive into my parents' split soon, but that's not what this chapter is about. This is the story of how I lost my virginity. Yup. Trigger warning: There's about to be gangly, awkward teenage sex.

After a few months of school year dating, Jake's and my parents grew sick of hauling us back and forth between each other's houses. Unwilling to let us drive ourselves, even though we had freshly minted licenses, they made the mutual decision to let us start having sleepovers—so long as we slept in separate rooms. Because, yeah. That was totally going to work.

Jake and I interpreted this new arrangement as a sign that we were ready to take the next step. To finally do "it." Like most teenagers, however, we had no concept of romance. Rather than lighting a few candles and letting the moment sweep us away, we planned the occasion to death. We consulted our friends and watched several R-rated movies so that we would "know what to do" when the time came. In essence, Jake and I were blind to the simple fact that excessive preparation often leads to excessive nervousness. (Mistake number one.)

We decided to lose our virginities on October 26, 2007, an auspicious date chosen mainly because my mom would be out with friends that night. (I also remember being very focused for some reason on not wanting to spend another Halloween as a virgin. Blame my not-yet-fully-formed brain for somehow linking the holiday with this momentous life decision.)

I was *so* nervous. In the days leading up to the deed, I thought about sex constantly. I obsessed over questions like: "Would it fit? Would it hurt? Is it true that you can't get pregnant if you shower straight after sex?"

In all our planning, the one thing Jake and I neglected to discuss was who would bring the condoms. That's how I ended up texting my soccer teammate Michelle just hours before, asking for a last minute favor. Michelle wasn't my best friend—or even a close friend, for that matter. But she did have her own car, which meant she could drive me to the CVS a few towns over to avoid running into my mom's friends with Trojans in hand. Michelle was a great chauffeur, but she was worthless when it came to condom selection. She merely shrugged and said she was a virgin herself. Ever the optimist and not understanding the product, I reached for the extrapleasure box instead of desensitizing. Because, duh. Who doesn't want more pleasure? (This was my second mistake, as teenage boys do not need *any* extra stimulation.)

I hid the condoms under the latest issue of *People* magazine, which featured the inside scoop behind Ryan Gosling and Rachel McAdams's breakup, and threw a cherry Blow Pop on top as a last-minute distraction from my primary purchase. The irony of this was not lost on me, even at the time.

"Big night?" the checkout girl asked with a gum smack as she accepted my twenty-dollar bill. I avoided her eyes, then hustled back to the safety of Michelle's minivan with my loot in hand.

When I returned, Jake was waiting on my front lawn looking about as nervous as I felt. He was a pale, trembly mess. We exchanged a chaste kiss hello, the air between us a thick cocktail of hormones and anxiety. *This was going to be so awkward*, I remember thinking at the time.

I have to admit that my childhood bedroom—with its toile wallpaper, baby blue carpet, and tiny twin bed—was a remarkably unsexy place. To make matters worse, all of the furniture was made out of white wicker, giving the space a summer-cottage-meets-haunted-dollhouse kind of vibe.

But Jake and I were teenagers, which meant that nothing—not even nuclear war—could kill our libidos. We were going to have sex whether Mystic the Unicorn Beanie Baby was watching or not.

Jake and I clambered onto the bed—insecure, aroused, and (for some reason) in a terrible rush. When I felt *it* happen, I closed my eyes and thought: *Hello, world. Danielle is officially here.*

Twenty-five seconds later, it was over. I stared at my glow-in-the dark-star-covered ceiling and thought about how relieved I was not to be a virgin anymore. Because you know the best thing about losing your virginity? It's a one-time thing. You never have to do it again. I could actually feel the weight of a thousand-pound gorilla named "childhood" lifting off my shoulders.

My sense of newfound maturity lasted approximately…twelve hours. Because as soon as Jake's parents picked him up the next morning, I began to feel nauseous. I decided that I was pregnant because, duh, morning sickness totally does start the next day and it couldn't possibly be the twenty-four-piece chicken nuggets I insisted on eating as a postcoital victory snack. (Mistake number three.)

So I did what all grown-ups do, and ran to my mother.

"Mom," I screamed as I burst into her room, interrupting her morning coffee. "Jake and I had sex. I'm pregnant and need the morning-after pill right now." In retrospect, probably among the worst and least scientifically accurate words a parent can hear.

I expected my mom to be furious. Instead, she merely smiled and set her mug on the nightstand. "Danielle," she said in her best

I'm-taking-you-seriously voice. "You *can* conceive while using a condom, but it's extremely unlikely that you would already be experiencing morning sickness. Are you absolutely sure that you're pregnant?"

I nodded my head. "I'm positive." Apparently both logic and everything I learned in health class flew out the window the second penis entered vagina.

I waited for my mom to freak out—to yell, to scream, to ground me from now to eternity. Instead, she merely laughed and gave me a congratulatory Jewish slap on the face. (There is a really weird tradition in Judaism where mothers lightly slap their daughters across the face when they get their first period. Please don't ask me to explain it.)

"All right then," she said, laughing, "you better get your pregnant tush in the car."

Together, we drove back to the same CVS (once again eager to avoid any awkward encounters). I walked in just as the same checkout girl was finishing her overnight shift. As we strode past her en route to the pharmacy, the girl noted my mom and asked me how I'd enjoyed the *People* magazine. "It was fine," I murmured as my mom looked on curiously.

I spent the rest of the day waiting for the moment when my mom's anger would commence, but the meltdown never came. Most moms would *freak out* when faced with the news that their only daughter had just lost her virginity. But Andrea Bernstein kept calm and carried on, which benefited our relationship in a number of ways—the most important of which was that it forged open lines of communication. After that experience, I was never afraid to share with my mother again. Sex, drugs, religion. Nothing is off the table.

It's funny. I would have thought the most important thing about losing my virginity would have been the actual penis-in-vagina. And the fact that I lost it to a loving boyfriend on my terms. And while, sure, that was a pretty epic milestone, what I remember most about that day is my mom's behavior. How she was able to set her own undeniably complicated emotions aside in order to be there and support me. To this day, I think about my mom whenever I'm faced with challenging news from a friend, employee, or lover. I channel her understanding and her calm. Why? Because maybe then that person won't hesitate to come to me in the future. Because anger is never, or almost never, the right reaction.

Some Questions Are Better Left Unanswered

Millennials are used to having everything at our fingertips. We loathe being in the dark, aching to answer every question with a quick search on our smartphone. And when Google isn't available…well, we're driven *insane*. My generation's thirst for information is both our best and worst quality—our best because we're always learning, and our worst because we don't know when to leave things alone.

Let's back up to the summer that I met Jake—the summer of my fourteenth birthday. When I returned to Long Island in August, everything seemed normal. Maybe I was still distracted from my first trip to second base, but my parents were happy. Or at least they seemed to be.

A few weeks later, I started my freshman year at Great Neck South. I joined the soccer team and threw myself into the high school social scene. But one day not long after, I came home to discover an odd scene: my entire family gathered silently in the living room. It was so quiet you could hear a pin drop. Immediately suspicious, I switched my Motorola Razr to silent and entered the room. "What's going on?" I asked, bracing for bad news. "Did someone die? Where are Grandma and Poppy?"

My questions hung in the air as I scanned my family for answers. Jack and Alec sat on opposite ends of the green velvet sofa where we had fallen asleep watching *Saturday Night Live* the night before. But today the TV was switched off, and there would be no smiles. Today, our parents—perched as far away from each other as possible—looked stoic and pale. Hell, even our pugs, Oscar and Felix, seemed poisoned by the toxic energy.

I may have been young, but I wasn't stupid. I knew that something must be seriously wrong in order to warrant this kind of meeting. (We were more of a dance-around-the-kitchen family than a sit-down-and-talk-about-feelings family.) Given how many of my friends' parents had gotten divorced in recent years, I could guess what I was about to be told. And I wasn't ready to accept it.

"Why don't you take a seat," my dad murmured, his tone confirming the severity of the situation. I looked at my brothers for help, but, being teenage boys, they avoided eye contact and exhibited no emotion whatsoever. It was at that moment I decided I was going to express enough feeling for all three siblings combined.

I threw myself onto the floor and thrashed as if having a seizure. "Please don't do this," I begged. "Don't say what you're about to say. We can fix this. We're still a family." I recited every line from whatever ABC drama I was watching at the time as memories of family road trips and winters spent in Puerto Rico flashed before my eyes.

My dad shook his head sadly. "I'm so sorry, Yelly, but this is happening. Your mother and I are separating." It was the first time I ever saw that six-feet-four giant of a man, who always seems so strong and confident, cry. As for me, I couldn't have been at a worse age—old enough to know my life would never be the same, but too young to fully comprehend the complexity of grown-up relationships.

The rest of the conversation was a blur. I remember my mom being very concerned that we not blame her for the separation. When I asked—*pleaded*—for an explanation, all she said was, "Daddy doesn't want to be married to Mommy anymore." (If my father had any issues with this approach, he didn't express them to us.)

Anticipating that we would be distraught, our parents had planned for each sibling to have a friend come over that evening. My BFF, Ashley, arrived an hour later. We lay beneath my baby blue comforter, Ashley stroking my hair while I cried. (Her parents are still together, but Ashley has a notoriously sympathetic ear.)

"Everything will be okay," she cooed softly as she tucked my bangs behind my ear. "Chelsea's parents are divorced, and look at her; she's totally fine."

But nothing Ashley said made me feel any better. I was just so shocked. I had *never* seen my parents fight. In fact, my only memories of their marriage were of my dad playfully slapping my mom on the butt while she cooked, or him whisking her away to an anniversary getaway upstate. They made an unbeatable charades team. There had been no visible precursors of the storm to come.

My parents should be nominated for an Academy Award, because it turns out they had spent the entire summer (while we were at our beloved Camp Birchmont) hammering out the details of their trial separation. My father had already rented an apartment. Only ten minutes away, he visited the house often whenever my mom wasn't home. My brothers would spend the occasional overnight at his new place, but I refused to see it. As long as I didn't set foot on the property, I thought, then it wasn't real. Typical kid stuff.

Being a relatively small suburb of just ten thousand residents, Great Neck is the perfect place to raise your children if you're looking for idyllic safety. But it's also the worst place if you're trying to avoid gossip. Everyone knows everyone's business, especially when the people at the heart of the scandal are the innocuous Bernsteins with their three all-star children and two adorable pups. Having never appeared on the drama circuit before, we were suddenly attracting all kinds of attention.

I began to suspect there was something I didn't know about my parents' relationship. A normal divorce wouldn't elicit this much interest. And so uncovering the reason for their separation became my sole mission. I pestered them both, but especially my mother, assuming she was the parent more likely to crack.

I'm not proud of it, but I tried to trick my mom into a confession on numerous occasions. I begged and pleaded, telling her it was the lack of information that made the situation so difficult. I asked:

What did Daddy do?
Do you still love him?
Is he ever coming back?

To her credit, my mom held her ground and refused to fall for my tricks. No matter what I asked, she always gave the same short response: "Daddy doesn't want to be married to Mommy anymore." And she left it at that.

We could all tell that mom was sugarcoating things. Something must have warranted the dissolution of our family. My brothers were happy to live in the dark, but I needed to know *what* had torn our family apart.

My investigation screeched to a halt, however, when I came home from soccer practice a few months later to find my dad sprawled on the couch watching golf. "Hi, Yelly," he called out, using his favorite nickname for me. "How was school?" And with that, he was back.

My dad moved home without pomp or circumstance. The explanation? That our parents had simply missed our family too much and decided to give things another shot. We accepted their words, had dinner at Peter Luger's steakhouse (where we always celebrated milestones), and things pretty much returned to normal.

My dad's return felt amazing. Like coming up for air after holding my breath too long under water—like the past two months had been a nightmare from which I'd finally woken up. I could unclench and relax. I could also suspend my amateur investigation, because the separation was over.

In my memory, things went back to the way they were. My parents continued not to fight. Dad flirted with mom in the kitchen. We spent the holidays with my grandparents down in Florida. If there were any lingering issues between my parents, I was either too happy or too young to ask about them. I saw everything through the rose-tinted glasses of a child desperate for her family's reunion.

Unfortunately, it was only a matter of months before my brothers and I were called back to the living room for *another* family meeting. This time, even the boys seemed to know what was happening before our parents spoke. I burst into tears and begged my parents not to do this to us. Again.

But Daddy was moving out. And this time there would actually be a *divorce*.

I reopened my investigation that very day. *Why had my parents split? Could I get them back together? Was a* Parent Trap *possible even if none of us had a British accent?*

In retrospect, it's obvious that I should have stopped harassing my parents and asked to see a therapist. But I was a dog driven mad by a bone. And if no one would tell me what happened, well, then, I was just going to have to employ more extreme measures.

I don't remember how the idea came to me, or how I could've been insane enough to try it, but I started listening to my mother's phone calls. This was the early 2000s, before the extinction of land-lines. Every night, my mom would retire to her room to call one of the women in her own family—either my Grandma Joyce or Aunt Amy. She told them everything.

What my mother didn't know is that while my room lacked a phone, it did have a phone jack. All I had to do was "borrow" a cordless phone from a friend's house, plug it in, and practice how to pick up so that it wouldn't make the giveaway click. Then, *bingo*. I could hear everything my mom said.

I was too young to understand a lot of it, but it seemed like my father was at fault. (Now, of course, I realize that no relationship is black and white.)

If there's one thing people should know about Danielle Bernstein, it's that she doesn't shy away from a confrontation. I'm not afraid to put things out in the open (hence this entire book). So, no. I didn't cry on my bathroom floor while I debated whether or how to confront my mother. Instead I ran straight to her room and demanded that she tell me what had happened. (I'm realizing now that I must have burst into my mother's room on a regular basis. But I digress.)

Still, my mom avoided spilling the deets. It wasn't until I graduated high school two years later that I finally got the answers I was looking for. My mom and I were driving in our family's Grand Cherokee, probably on our way to splurge on Häagen-Dazs. I don't know if it was the fact that I had recently turned eighteen or that I was headed to college in a few short months, but for some reason *this* was the day that my mom decided to start sharing.

Out of respect for my family's privacy, I won't get into the details. What I will say is this: my dad was, and continues to be, a great father. But as a spouse, he had room to grow.

To my own surprise, as my mom finally explained how things fell apart, all I wanted to do was plug my ears. I had been so desperate to understand what had happened to my parents' marriage. Now that I knew, however, it only made me more upset. (My mom, on the other hand, seemed relieved to have finally been able to share.)

I walked away from that conversation with the answers I had craved for so long. But I also finally realized…those answers only left me with more questions.

Can I trust men?
Should my mom really be telling me this?
Why didn't I just leave things alone?

More than ten years later, I am still actively working to heal the wounds of my parents' divorce. I have devastating trust issues. And since trust is critical in all relationships—whether they be platonic, romantic, or professional—my hesitance to have faith in people can be a serious handicap. Just ask any of my ex-boyfriends. The divorce severely warped my sense of love and monogamy. It took me years of therapy to learn how to behave in romantic relationships, how to not automatically assume the worst. And there's still a long road before me.

As for my mother, that was the day she stopped just seeing me as her daughter and started seeing me as her friend. It completely changed our relationship and took years of therapy together to get back to a healthy balance of the two. I became angry at her, angry at my dad, angry at the situation.

In retrospect, I wish I had never launched my teenage investigation into my parents' breakup. I wish I could unknow what my mom told me that day in her Jeep Cherokee. More than anything, though, I wish I had been more careful what I asked for. What I thought I needed to know. Because, as I've come to learn—more than once, it turns out—some questions truly are better left unanswered.

Money Doesn't Buy Style

I grew up on Long Island's Gold Coast, an area known for its extravagant wealth, opulent estates, and ever expanding population of Range Rovers. Great Neck is the kind of place where the student loan crisis doesn't seem to exist. Where the average price per bar mitzvah rivals that of the royal wedding. (Meghan, not Kate. We're not *insane*.)

Compared to the rest of the world, I had an extremely privileged upbringing. My dad had the same great job then that he has today as the chief operating officer of a large staffing and recruitment agency in Manhattan. My mom enjoyed a career in advertising before retiring to care for us kids. We lived in a comfortable bubble, and it wasn't until I was older that I knew anything otherwise. But compared to my classmates, my family wasn't considered "rich"—in a neighborhood of six-thousand-square-foot mansions, our one-story ranch looked practically modest.

My fellow high schoolers looked like they'd strutted off the pages of *Seventeen* magazine, decked out in designer brands my parents refused to buy on account of them being "a waste of money." Like any status-conscious, self-conscious teenager circa 2010, I was desperate for Juicy tracksuits and True Religion jeans. (Of course, it's true that teenagers have no business spending $60 on a T-shirt, but at the time I would have literally traded everything in my closet for a single sweater bedazzled with the word JUICY on it.)

Then came the divorce. After my parents' split, they had two households to support, each one large enough for one adult, three children, and two pugs. Fortunately, my mom didn't have to sell the house, but there was the typical, postsplit belt tightening.

My mom had always loved taking my brothers and me on regular shopping trips to the local department stores. It was one of the many ways we bonded. Now, in an effort to pare back expenses, she implemented a new mandate: the Bernstein children were now responsible for picking their own clothes. We would be given money to shop once per season and were required to get everything we needed in that single haul. Anything beyond those parameters would have to be bought and paid for ourselves.

The small budget given to each of us was totally workable, except during teenage growth spurts. (I was five-feet-two at the start of my freshman year and five-feet-eight at graduation.) I wish ankle jeans had been on trend at the time, because I spent most of high school with pants that were just a little too short.

My brothers hated this new way of shopping. Desperate to get home, they developed the habit of walking into a store and grabbing the first thing they saw. I, however, loved the responsibility that came with my mom's mandate. Finally, I was in the driver's seat of my own closet. If I liked a skirt that didn't abide by the "fingertip rule," I could buy it without asking for my mom's permission. Hell, I even loved the restriction of shopping on a budget. I had to think extrahard about how I'd wear each piece, keeping versatility top of mind. It forced me to plan outfits in a way I never would have otherwise (which, for those who haven't noticed, paid off a few years later).

While my brothers viewed these shopping trips as (at best) character building and (at worst) a sick form of torture, I saw them as a step toward adulthood. Planning and buying a capsule collection for myself each season was *fun*—like an extended-play version of my morning dressing routine. It made me feel incredibly grown-up.

Things got even better when I discovered Century 21. A Brooklyn mainstay since 1961, Century 21's department stores are one of the most popular discount fashion chains in the Tristate Area. Think of it as our local version of Nordstrom Rack or TJ Maxx.

Most people love Century 21 because it's affordable, but just as many hate it because their stores are huge and as well organized as my family's junk drawer. Racks are jammed with the marked-down spoils of seasons past. Shelves overflow with off-brand underwear wrapped in plastic. Dressing rooms burst with whatever the person before you left inside. And don't get me started on the smell.

If there's a method to Century 21's madness, most casual shoppers can't discern it. But I have never been a casual shopper.

Given the level of thought I put into my wardrobe, my quarterly budget was more than enough to supply me with a season's worth of haul. There were fashion finds to be discovered at stores like Century 21; all you needed was the drive and patience to dig for them. The entire operation was an exciting scavenger hunt—an opportunity to spend an entire day tracking down hidden gold, like Splendid rollover leggings on sale for half off. In retrospect, my taste for vintage shopping should come as no surprise, as I've clearly always gotten off on the thrill of the hunt.

When I got a little bit older, I'd shop at Macy's. Oh, Macy's—some of my fondest high school memories were spent speeding down Community Drive into the Manhasset parking lot, those big red letters beckoning me like a moth to the flame. I'd go alone, remain focused, and find a head-turning outfit for whatever high school party I was attending that weekend. I'll never forget waking up on the morning of prom, only to realize that my matching shoes had become a chew toy for our dogs. I knew there was only one place where I was guaranteed to find something that matched so last minute. I sped to Macy's, found perfect nude heels (on sale too), and made it to my hair appointment in the nick of time.

My future career as a designer was already taking root back then too. My strapped-for-cash teenage self would often take apart clothes and resew pieces to keep her closet fresh. Of course, I was no seamstress, but a family friend had taught me the basics of hand sewing. I could reinvent my clothes by cutting them up and reshaping them with safety pins, too, no expert needlework required.

I remember being so excited each night before I got to wear a new outfit to school that I would have trouble falling asleep. I'd lay awake fantasizing about the next morning, when I'd strut through the main hall at Great Neck South like it was a catwalk. Sure, I didn't have the latest bag from Dooney & Bourke. But even if I wasn't going to win points for designer labels, I was damn sure going to win for creativity.

Come junior year, I had outgrown my mother's budget. It was time to take matters into my own hands and get a job. There was no question where I would work: Great Neck Plaza. More specifically, for this twenty-five-year-old girl named Naomi who managed a new boutique called Apparel Addiction. To me, she seemed like the only person in this otherwise bougie suburb who appreciated high fashion. (Plus, there was the fact that working at Apparel Addiction would guarantee me an employee discount at a store I couldn't otherwise afford.)

I marched in, my impossibly short résumé in hand. "I'd like a job."

"Okay. But why should I hire you?" I remember Naomi asking. "No offense, but you have no experience."

"Because if you don't hire me, someone else will," I replied with all the bravado I could muster, feeling her gaze take in my outfit's unusual (but genius!) mix of plaid and leopard prints.

I got the job and started that day.

Apparel Addiction sold contemporary clothes to a young clientele. Most of our customers were women in their twenties, or teenagers who came in with their mothers looking for something specific, like a dress for the high school dance. Because I was roughly the same age as many of our shoppers, I soon found myself doing a lot more than folding sweaters and cleaning out dressing rooms. I became an impromptu stylist, helping customers create looks for particular occasions. And I *loved* it.

People started asking for me by name, saying they had driven from thirty minutes away so that I could dress them for some event. I had regulars who would call and ask me to pull selections before they arrived. It was my first chance to exercise the creativity and attention to detail that I used when creating my own outfits. At one point I started to realize…I was pretty freaking great at this.

Every once in a while, Naomi would let me take home clothes that were damaged or unsold. These items were usually ripped, flawed, or covered in someone else's foundation, requiring me to bust out my needle and thread before transforming them into something wearable. I spent weeks on the carpeted floor of my bedroom, cutting up clothes and hand stitching them back together. My entire senior year was dedicated to the mission of creating the world's most flattering tube skirt. (Turns out, a flattering tube skirt doesn't exist.)

My grandmother Joyce seemed to take special notice that, for me, fashion was more than a shopping habit. Joyce is the kind of woman who, at eighty-seven years old, still refuses to leave her house without a full face of makeup. She's got style and knows good tailoring when she sees it. On my last Hanukkah before college, she gifted me an old sewing machine. As soon as I unwrapped it, I started begging my parents for spring sewing classes at the Fashion Institute of Technology in the city. I wanted to learn how fashion professionals made clothes so that my amateur alterations could look more refined. My parents finally relented—probably thinking those few weeks of classwork would keep me out of trouble. (The joke was on them.)

If I hadn't needed to sew my own clothes, would I be able to design my own pieces today? For that matter, would I still have founded *WeWoreWhat* if I hadn't been such a bargain shopper, always scouting how to get the look for less? Would I have developed a sense of style that was both chic and functional if I hadn't been forced to think strategically about my closet?

I'll never know, but I can say this (as cheesy as it sounds): just as money can't buy happiness, it also can't buy style. Those early trips to department stores taught me that first-rate fashion can be found at any price point. It's a mantra I continue to preach on my platform every day by mixing high- and low-end brands. Because, you see, style isn't a thing; it isn't hanging on the hooks waiting for you to purchase it. It's about knowledge and taste, about knowing what suits you best. Real style is a free combination of creativity, patience, and most of all, self-confidence.

The Importance of Bitch Work

Despite being raised in Long Island suburbia, I was born to be a city girl. Always itching to be at the heart of things, I spent the majority of my high school years inventing reasons to go into Manhattan. I rode the Long Island Railroad from Great Neck to Penn Station so many times, in fact, that I can still hear the conductor's voice as he announced the name and order of every stop. "Stand clear of the closing doors, please."

Oh, how I used to love that commuter train. It didn't matter if the person sitting next to me spent the entire forty-five minutes screaming into their Blackberry about their au pair's insane choice to feed the kids Kraft Mac & Cheese instead of quinoa. Because with every blurry suburb that passed my window and every skyscraper that came into view, I knew I was one step closer to New York City.

To me, New York has always been the center of the universe. The Big Apple. The hub of every industry from fashion to finance to real estate. I came out of the womb needing, craving, to be a part of it. The energy, the hustle, the sense of possibility—it's like an environment tailor-made for my neurotic psyche. (I love a Hamptons weekend as much as the next girl, but the bustle of Manhattan is where I thrive.)

By my sixteenth birthday, I managed to convince a few of my more adventurous friends to start coming with me to sneak into clubs. My Camp Birchmont bunkmate Ashley was nervous but persuadable. There was no question that both Chelsea and Adriana were in too. (They were my more "advanced" friends.)

Almost every Friday of our upper class years, the four of us would pack our fake IDs and don our shortest skirts. Using water bottles full of Bacardi Razz, we would pregame on the train into the city. I remember feeling so adult, though to anyone sitting around us we surely looked like the children we were. (If only every inch of heel I wore added a year to my age, I could have been twenty-one.)

Our destinations were usually Pink Elephant, Kiss and Fly, or one of the other now defunct clubs on the West Side of Manhattan. Particularly the Chelsea and Meatpacking neighborhoods, with their cavernous buildings and cobblestone streets, were once the center of New York's nightlife. (It's why *SatC*'s Samantha chose to buy her first apartment there.)

West Twenty-Seventh Street in particular was known as "Club Row" due to the sheer number of venues on the block. Most of the places I frequented back then have since closed, following in the footsteps of other famously deceased discotheques like Tunnel, Bungalow 8, and Studio 54. The only 2000s club that still remains is Marquee, from which the party has moved on these days unless a famous DJ is visiting. So many of my formerly favorite clubs are now populated by the bridge-and-tunnel crowd—suburbanites who come looking for authentic New York nightlife, but find only themselves. (Of course we were B&T, too, back then, but we thought nobody noticed.)

The early 2000s was also the era of club promoters, a.k.a. good-looking men who trolled the city for even better-looking women whom they could bring to clubs. If it sounds sketchy, that's because it was. But it was also the easiest way for a bunch of underage high schoolers to get into a club without having to spend a dime of their own money.

Our favorite promoter was Chris, whom we met one night outside of Cane Nightclub while I was (per usual) refusing to wait in line. I marched straight up to the doorman in my platform wedges and demanded that my friends and I be let in. Right. Now. I'm lucky we were a group of cute young girls—otherwise someone probably would have punched me in the face.

The doorman called over Chris, who happened to be the club's promoter that night. And thus began a mutually beneficial friendship. Chris would take my friends and me to free dinners at various trendy restaurants around the city, our favorite of which was TAO. Then, we'd get a table at whatever club he was working that night. Of course, we were underage, but let's just say that most New York businesses look the other way when pretty young things order a cocktail. Soon, talking my way out of lines became a thing of the past. I did, however, find myself missing my frequent conversations with Sal, the bald doorman I befriended at Pink Elephant. (Sal, if you're reading this, please DM me. I miss you.)

At the end of the night, my girls and I would race back to Penn Station and catch the 3:19 a.m. train to Great Neck just as the doors were closing. If we missed it, we'd have to wait until 5:19 a.m. No way we could shell out $70 for a cab. But if we caught the train, we got to enjoy the social scene that was the LIRR itself.

The 3:19 a.m. train was like something out of a movie. Every cool teenager from the north shore of Long Island was on it, congregating for forty-five more minutes of parent-free debauchery. Observers from every generation have shared stories about their own clandestine, late-night train rides home from Manhattan. And while my experience was a lot less glamorous than, say, Truman Capote's, the vibe was similar. The train was littered with high schoolers dressed in their edgiest outfits, reeking of alcohol and sweat. Most people were either still drinking or half asleep. The energy from the night still clung to us even as we sped back to our childhood homes. We were a tight-knit society that consisted not of varsity football players, but of the artsy kids, the thespians, the fashionistas. The people who, like me, were anxious to start their adult lives.

So when a family friend offered me a summer internship at G-III, a clothing company based in midtown Manhattan, I leaped at the opportunity to have an aboveboard reason to be in the city. G-III owns brands from Calvin Klein to Tommy Hilfiger to Levi's. I imagined myself working in a chic office space, playing a critical role supporting fashion executives as they did important work. While my friends fell into jobs as lifeguards or babysitters, I could make my first real foray into the fashion industry.

This internship seemed like the moment I could say goodbye to the old Danielle (who thought cocktails were best served in a Solo cup) and hello to the new, more cosmopolitan me (who would drink martinis straight up with an olive and wear those shoes with the fancy red bottoms). I would be a real Manhattan girl.

On my first day, I arrived at G-III's midtown offices ready to be the best damn intern the women's coats and dresses department had ever seen. I wondered what I was going to do that day. How long would it be until my first photo shoot? When I would get to have lunch at Balthazar? How long it would be until I met any celebrities? (It didn't have to be anyone *crazy* famous. Leighton Meester would suffice.)

My daydreams were interrupted when my new boss appeared in the lobby. Diane was a forty-something firecracker, the kind of New York woman who walked with purpose and invariably hid her five-feet-two stature by wearing a knockout pair of stilettos. (Aquazurra was her favorite brand.) She barely looked up from her Blackberry, but I could already tell she had been in fashion forever and was likely the sole owner of a prewar apartment on the Upper East Side.

"Are you Danielle?" Diane asked, and I nodded. "Great. I'll show you to your office."

I expected Diane to lead me to my own desk or at least some sort of communal workspace, but instead she took me straight to…a closet? She explained that my job for the day was to steam rack after rack of trench coats, then pin them to a blank wall for someone to come in and photograph.

Anyone hoping to pursue a career in fashion must pay extra attention to this next paragraph: at some point in every young fashionista's life, she will have to intern in a fashion closet. If you're lucky, it will at least be at either Hearst or a cubicle at Condé Nast. Somewhere with high-end brands and (a girl can dream) a window. Most fashion closets, however, are the size of Harry Potter's original bedroom and about half as nice. The one upside is that the lack of daylight is exceptionally comforting when recovering from a hangover, not that most people interning are old enough to get them.

Occasional breaks will be permitted if you're doing one of two things: fetching coffee or running samples around town. (Diane took a medium almond milk latte from Gregory's.) I thought I would start that internship by getting to shadow the buyers' appointments or visiting showrooms. Instead, I got a reality check.

I could amuse you with tales from that summer. I could tell you how I spent entire days tracking samples in an Excel spreadsheet or about the time I tried to carry $20,000 worth of dresses on the subway to a Kate Bosworth photoshoot. (Condé Nast interns, of course, got black cars.) The real excitement came when freebies were dumped onto the counter in the office kitchen. The editors picked first, then the assistants, and finally the interns. We would launch a full-on *Lord of the Flies* battle over a pair of cowboy boots that had appeared in last month's *Elle*.

Even so, I wouldn't trade a goddamn second of that summer. Sure, it was boring. Sure, I was a glorified (and unpaid) personal assistant. But bitch work is a time-honored tradition in the fashion industry—spending months, or even years, doing manual labor is a prerequisite for any of the more glamorous jobs. During these moments, you learn not to complain. That the tedious work has to be done by someone, and every single person on the ladder above you has already done it. You aren't entitled to a position because you shadowed someone for two weeks at *Teen Vogue* or because you're from a rich family. There is no immediate gratification in a fashion career. Not for anyone. And that's *good*.

My stint at G-III also taught me that the bottom is the place in the industry where you're encouraged to ask a lot of questions. Where you can learn (and screw up occasionally) without the real threat of being fired. There's room to grow, and not a whole lot to lose, since you're not a paid employee. Take advantage of it.

I interact with ambitious people who want to make it big in fashion all the time—hell, I'm one of them. But I think my generation, and Gen Z even more, has been warped to crave instant gratification. Not everyone seems able to accept the necessity of hard work, or that good things take time. They don't realize that people who expect things to be handed to them don't make it in the long run, or understand the concept that even with hard work, success isn't guaranteed. I've encountered this most when hiring for *WeWoreWhat*. And what we all need, at least once in a while, is the kind of attitude adjustment that comes with a nice, lowly internship. As for me, whenever I feel myself getting a big head, I simply remind myself that I'm "Danielle, the fashion closet intern."

Make the First Move

For better or worse, I've never been shy. I also never really understood that old advice to "Let him chase you," or "Don't come on too strong," or "Let him make the first move." What's the point of that? I've been the initiator in at least half, if not more, of my romantic relationships.

You have to just go after what you want. And sometimes what you want is the boy you're not supposed to have.

The year was 2009. The month, early May. I was a couple of weeks into my G-III internship when, one day, Diane came to visit me in the closet—a.k.a. the only room small enough to make her look tall. She was there to lecture me about the *"very good-looking young man"* who had started with the company that day.

"G-III has strict rules about fraternization, especially when it comes to interns," she explained. "So I'm chatting with all you girls."

That was Diane's first mistake. Anyone who has met me knows that you can't tell me not to do something, because then I *have* to do it. I'm the kid and the cookie jar.

Michael was twenty-one at the time, which made him several years my senior. He was a recent graduate of Syracuse University in upstate New York—a snow globe masquerading as a school—and was hired to build G-III's e-commerce website. What can I say? He was a bright tech nerd with the looks of a Ralph Lauren model. And I was toast.

I'll never forget the first moment I saw Michael. I was talking to Diane—a.k.a. listening to her rant about how Goyard had dared to back-order her new handbag—when he strolled off the elevator. It's cheesy, but I'm not joking when I say time stood still. I barely managed to pull my jaw off the floor as I gave him the world's longest once-over.

People already know that I'm a fan of tall, dark, and handsome. It's not something I do consciously, but I have a type. According to both my friends and my old Instagram photos, I only date guys who are over six-feet-three, have dark hair, and sport a groomed, but still scruffy, beard. (The beard is a key component.) And if they happen to be sporting a well-worn leather jacket…well, all the better.

The only issue with Michael, despite our coworker status, was that we were temporarily on opposite sides of our eighteenth birthdays. I became legal on May 28, which made me straight-up jailbait for another few weeks. Anything that transpired between Michael and me would be a crime, at least for the time being.

Was it too much to expect that I could convince this guy to break both the law and company rules? Challenge accepted.

The next day, I gussied myself up in my favorite J Brand jeans (high rise, ankle cut), a Splendid tank top, and a black BCBG blazer draped over my shoulders. It was the perfect sexy yet casual yet professional look in which I exuded confidence without revealing too much skin. (This is a delicate balance perhaps best exemplified by every French woman on the planet.)

When I entered the office, I made sure to strut past Michael's desk without introducing myself. (Keep in mind this was only his second day, so he had barely met anyone.) My behavior *might* have seemed rude…if it weren't for the fact that I eye-fucked his brains out while walking past. (Hey, the tactic worked with my first boyfriend back at Camp Birchmont. Why couldn't the same tactic work here?)

Unfortunately, Michael didn't take the bait. I did catch him staring at me a few times throughout the workday when he thought I wasn't looking, but he didn't utter so much as a word to me. When a coworker finally did introduce us (beside the sacred Keurig machine in the break room), Michael smiled politely and shook my hand like he'd never seen me before in his life. That's when I realized if I wanted something to happen, I needed to be more direct.

That evening, I schemed the entire train ride back to Great Neck. *Should I cut the bullshit and ask him out? Or should I play it cool? Would asking him to live together be considered "too much, too soon?"*

By the time I passed Bayside, Queens, I had a plan. After family dinner, I raced to my room with a pen and a stack of Post-Its. The rest of my evening was spent coming up with the perfect "straightforward but casual" note for me to leave on Michael's desk the next day.

In the end, I decided to keep things simple with just my name and number—a clean, classic approach. Michael would know I was interested without me having asked for anything specific. (Nailing the perfect handwriting for my message, however, took another hour. I've never been the kind of girl who was good at penmanship.)

I waited all day to make my move, so I could leave the office immediately in case it went horribly wrong. At 4:55 p.m. I strolled past Michael's desk without so much as a glance in his general direction. But then just as I was about to turn a corner, I whipped the Post-It note out of my pocket and stuck the thing boldly to his computer screen. Mission accomplished.

So what did I do next? I ran to the bathroom, hid in a stall, and called Ashley. "*What?*" she screamed, louder than was necessary. "I can't believe you did that!"

Ten minutes later, I emerged from the bathroom with Ashley's advice to "act like nothing happened" fresh in my ears. I packed up my things and left.

That night on the train, I was certain that I had made a serious mistake—been too forward, embarrassed a colleague, committed an offense that would see me fired from my first internship. I very rarely question my actions, but this was a moment of real introspection. Perhaps my straightforward candor, which had worked in high school, was too much for the adult world.

Turns out, Michael was merely waiting until after work to reach out. His first text arrived just after 6:00 p.m., as the New York skyline was fading into the distance outside my train's window. I had to read his words six times before I could internalize them. "That was smooth. Saturday night drinks at Soho House?—Michael."

My ego did backflips.

Once I stopped celebrating, it was time to decipher the message. Soho was a neighborhood in Lower Manhattan—that I knew. That Soho *House* was an elite, members-only club in the Meatpacking District required a quick Google search. Sure, I snuck into the city all the time. I *thought* I knew the nightlife scene. But in reality, the clubs my friends and I frequented weren't the kind of places where real New Yorkers hung out. I was still just a wannabe suburbanite.

I spent a second consecutive night hiding in my bedroom, reading every article I could find about Soho House. (I hate to be underprepared and needed to know what to wear, how to act, etc.) I discovered that Soho House was not only a private club that admitted only members and their guests, but it also famously preferred artsy folks over finance-y New Yorkers. Hell, it even said they won't let you inside if you were wearing a suit. (They also disallow photos, a rule that would later get me kicked out from the venue. But let's not get into *that*.)

I was more than intimidated. So what did I do? I texted Michael that, yes, I was in, but maybe we should each bring a friend? Still a typical teenager, I instinctively wanted the safety of numbers. I'm sure Michael was too old for this approach to dating, but he obliged. And that's how I ended up on the phone with my friend Liza, begging her to spend Friday night in the city. ("Who goes out at nine?" I remember her asking. "I'm usually in bed by then.")

Liza was the perfect person for this kind of outing—a good kid who had been raised by parents as lenient as mine. Thank God, Liza accepted the invitation and agreed to tell her parents she was sleeping at my place. (I, of course, told my mother the opposite.)

Cut to the next night. She arrived at my house around four, and we spent hours getting ready. I kid you not, we were able to listen to Taylor Swift's entire *Fearless* album two full times before we were ready to go, our hair blown out and our water bottles full of cheap wine.

Liza and I were ripe with liquid courage by the time we crossed the cobblestones of Ninth Avenue and announced ourselves to the model-esque hostess at the front desk. (Just what you need before a first date: to be confronted with a woman who looks just like Megan Fox, only taller and with even bigger boobs.) After several clicks on a computer, she confirmed our names were on the list.

She coolly pointed toward the elevator and said, "Your host is waiting on the roof."

My anxiety dissipated as soon as I entered the elevator. The space was dark and moody, with pulsing music and leather-padded walls. Its glamour, however, was nothing compared to what we saw when the doors parted a few seconds later. "Are we in heaven?" Liza asked as we stepped onto the open-air terrace.

She wasn't wrong: it was the coolest place I'd ever seen. There were 360-degree views of the Manhattan skyline, including the reaches of the Empire State Building and the depths of the Hudson River. String lights hung above black-and-white striped furniture. The employees looked like movie stars, which no doubt they were striving to be during the day.

The only people better-looking than the servers were the actual celebrities. I tried not to stare at John Mayer as my eyes scanned the space for Michael, whom we spotted lounging on a daybed with his friend Pete. Damn, did Michael look good. He always wore T-shirts in the office, but this night his V-neck was a little deeper, his jeans a little tighter, his beard a little scruffier. If you'd thrown a distressed leather jacket over his shoulders, he would have been my dream man. (Even still with a suede bomber jacket, he was pretty close.)

Pete instantly charmed Liza, which was good because I started ignoring her as soon as I saw Michael smile. (Ah, the delicate dance of the teenage female friendship.) All I remember is alternating my gaze between Michael's stubble and the twinkling skyline, thinking, *Someone pinch me, please, so I know it's not a dream.*

Michael was a beautiful storyteller. I could (and did) spend hours listening to him recount stories from his twenty-one years of life. He seemed so worldly: not only had he already gone to college, but he'd also studied abroad *and* traveled to India and other faraway places. (My family's vacations to visit my grandparents in Florida suddenly lost their luster in comparison.)

Michael was born and raised in Manhattan. He could name all the trendy neighborhoods in Brooklyn and had seen the inside of the impossible-to-enter Gramercy Park. In other words, he was born to the kind of life that I was so intent on creating for myself.

Around midnight, he suggested that we leave Soho House and go clubbing. We ended up at 1 Oak, a classic New York club, one of the few of that era that still remain open. The club has giant bouncers, velvet ropes, and a line that always snaked around the block. (Pro tip: Grab a slice from Artichoke Pizza to enjoy while you wait. Unless you're wearing a bodycon dress, in which case you can't risk the bloat.)

Michael, of course, strolled straight to the front of the line and hugged one of the doormen. The ropes disappeared, the door swung open, and we were ushered inside. My eyes were blinded by the neon sign and the white tiled floor. I saw Justin Theroux at a table in the corner. *Toto, we aren't in Great Neck anymore.*

After a crazy evening at 1 Oak, we visited another downtown institution: The Diner, a great restaurant on the corner of

Fourteenth Street and Ninth Avenue, which has (*sob*) since closed. The joint stayed open twenty-four hours a day, luring the drunk, stoned, and hungry with its promise of Denver omelets. If you sauntered in after midnight, you were sure to see New York's crème de la crème—models, magazine editors, investment bankers—stuffing egg sandwiches into their faces and looking a hell of a lot less glamorous under the fluorescent lighting. (Thankfully, I was still young enough not to have concealer caked in my crow's feet, which is a constant struggle these days.)

As I ate my chicken tenders, I couldn't help but wonder why Michael—this smart, cultured older guy—was into me. Danielle. The Long Island girl who still rushed home every Thursday to watch *Grey's Anatomy* with her mom. I felt so…intimidated. And also desperate to be more like him.

Naturally, we missed the 3:19 a.m. train. And then the 5:19 a.m. train. Michael eventually suggested that the four of us take a cab to his apartment on the Upper West Side. That way Liza and I could catch a few hours of sleep before the LIRR started back up in the morning.

Turns out, Michael and I had one big thing in common: we both lived with our mothers. If before Michael had seemed a little too perfect, out of my league, we were now on a more level playing field. And that only attracted me further.

Michael told us what to expect as he slid his key in the door. "My mom's a pretty heavy sleeper, but she usually wakes up around now. She's cool, though. Don't worry." He may have been living at home like me, but as the door swung open I instantly recognized that this childhood home was nothing like mine. This was no ranch house in the suburbs. Michael's home was a classic six in a prewar, doorman building. Its massive windows had unobstructed views of Central Park. Expensive-looking artwork hung on the walls. Oriental rugs covered the floor. The entire space screamed *old money* and *culture.*

"Do you want a tour?" Michael asked as he emerged from the kitchen with four beers in hand. I accepted the offer, but Pete and Liza declined (opting to make out on the park-front balcony instead).

He loved the building's historic details—it's quintessential *New York*-ness. He led me from room to room, explaining that he'd spent his entire life in this very apartment. We admired its high ceilings, crown moldings, original hardwood floors, and still-functioning wood-burning fireplace. The only thing more charming than the oak built-ins was Michael's clear pride in his home.

When we reached his bedroom, Michael skipped the lights and led me to the window. He pointed east—over the park, over the skyscrapers that kept Long Island out of view. "So you live somewhere over there?" he asked. I nodded, and then he kissed me. Long, slow, and deep. Never again would I settle for kissing a teenager.

After that night, our summer devolved into one steamy fuck session. Michael and I would sneak off during our lunch break to have sex in his apartment while his mom was at work. We tried to keep the relationship secret from our coworkers, timing our departures to be at least five minutes apart. Michael kept inventing projects that required him to spend time in the fashion closet with me. There was the time I accidentally returned to work with my shirt inside out and a suspicious stain on my chest. (Ashley had a very different, more scandalized reaction when I called her from the bathroom that time.)

Turns out, sneaking around is freaking *hot*, especially when you're a new eighteen-year-old without much in the way of sexual experience. But what Michael and I had was more than sex. If I had sat down to imagine my perfect boyfriend, I couldn't have come up with a person more ideal than Michael. If my internship at G-III was the job that was going to make me a woman, then my relationship with Michael was meant to do the same.

Michael was my first true love. No question. (Sorry, Jake.) He was a savvy older man who showed me a version of New York I didn't yet know. He took me to the Brooklyn Bowl for indie concerts, to the Bowery Hotel for late night drinks. On low-key nights, he liked to frequent hole-in-the-wall restaurants. We traveled to Queens for great Greek food and the Bronx for this one dish "I had to try."

By the time August rolled around, my lust was turning to panic. I was leaving for college in just a few weeks. Would someone like Michael want to be in a relationship with a college freshman? But the more I doubted his attachment to me, the more he seemed attached.

Sometimes I think about what my life would be like if I hadn't written that Post-It. If I'd never made the first move. Michael introduced me to a world outside the bubble of Great Neck. I fell in love with him, but also in doing so, New York City. A life in the suburbs was no longer an option.

I took a risk and pursued a boy without fear of rejection. It's something that I've done so many times since—not just in my love life, but also in my work. I go after what I want, taking charge to create my own destiny. I don't wait for things to come to me; I make them happen. And it always serves me well.

Face the Path of Most Resistance

Most high schoolers apply to at least a dozen colleges, afraid that they might end up without any options. I, however, only applied to two: New York University and the University of Wisconsin in Madison. Both great universities, but they couldn't be more different. One is a liberal arts school in Lower Manhattan, famous for its celebrity students and urban campus. The other is a quintessential Big Ten school with a football team and badger mascot to boot.

I spent my senior year wrestling with the question: Where should I go to college? The decision was so momentous that it paralyzed me. Should I move to Manhattan, fill my life with internships, and launch full speed ahead into my adult life? Or was this my one chance to have an all-American college experience? Ever the Gemini, the uncertainty tore me apart.

I was accepted to NYU early decision, which meant a choice had to be made before hearing back from Wisconsin. It was entirely possible that I could decline NYU, not get into Wisconsin, and then end up totally screwed. I'd have to spend yet another semester at my mom's house, taking online courses and waiting to apply again.

I knew the risk I was facing, but I just couldn't pull the trigger on NYU. If the plan was to spend my adult life in Manhattan, then was this my only chance to try living somewhere new? The goal had always been to move to New York, be a New Yorker, live happily ever after, the end. But would I really be happy moving there at the tender age of eighteen, never to leave again?

I decided to turn down NYU and roll the dice on a Wisconsin acceptance. My friends were shocked. How could Danielle Bernstein, the girl who seized every chance to sneak into the city, say no to life in Manhattan? Maybe I'd watched too many episodes of the show *Greek*, which painted college as a four year holiday from real life, but my desire for the college experience won out.

After saying no to NYU, I lived every day in panic. I was terrified. So I cannot even begin to describe the weight that lifted off my shoulders the day my mom called to say a letter had arrived from the University of Wisconsin—the *big* kind. I was at soccer practice when the call came. I barreled toward my friends on the field and screamed, "I'm going to be a cheesehead," as we tumbled into the grass.

I flew to Madison in August, fresh faced and ready to take college head-on. I set out to get the most out of my experience: I immediately slept with the hottest senior guy (mistake), gained ten pounds in the dining hall (mistake), and attended (a.k.a. blacked out at) my first football game (#winning). I also attended my fair share of "GI Joes and army hoes" parties. You know, normal college stuff.

My dorm room was a suite—two shared bedrooms connected by a miniscule bathroom that hadn't been renovated since 1959. My assigned roommates—Sam, Jackie, and Peri—and I became fast friends the way you do when you don't really have a choice. We even decided to rush the same sorority (Sigma Delta Tau) a few weeks into the school year. I became the youngest social chair of the sorority, organizing all the parties and events.

I'd spend hours every night on G-Chat with Michael, but we had agreed to keep things casual while I was away. I had complete freedom to spend my first semester of college dating other guys. And since two is always better than one, I found two beaus who unfortunately happened to live in the same dorm—Elliot on the thirteenth floor and Ben on the first. (How those boys didn't find out about each other, I'll never know.)

Even though my social life in Madison was top notch, my classes definitely weren't—not because Wisconsin isn't a great school, but because they lack a true fashion program. I chose the closest thing and became a retail major. (If I never read another book on supply chain management, I'll die happy.)

As for extracurriculars, I found the college's only fashion club: Threads. The group meant twice a month with the sole purpose of curating an annual fashion show, with clothes donated from local boutiques. (Thank God Shopbop is headquartered in Madison, or I don't know what we would have done.) But Threads was like a Band-Aid for a bullet wound—not enough to satisfy a fashion fiend like me.

When I asked the head of my program about internships, she explained that a lot of retail majors enjoyed internships at the Kohl's, whose offices were located in nearby Menomonee Falls, Wisconsin. There's nothing wrong with Kohl's, but it wasn't exactly my dream employer. I wanted to intern at Chanel, not a department store.

Then it was time to fly home for winter break. I spent the first few nights at my mom's house before heading into the city for a long weekend at Chelsea's new apartment. Remember my old high school pal Chelsea? After graduation, she enrolled at the Fashion Institute of Technology. She rented a walk-up apartment in a postwar building on the Lower East Side. Sure, the place was a shithole. She had more mice than roommates. But as I listened to Chelsea describe nights spent clubbing at The Darby (now famously renamed Up&Down) and days spent vintage shopping in the East Village, I felt a fierce tug of jealousy. That was supposed to be me. It was the first inkling that maybe my life had gotten off track.

A few days later, I met Michael for an overnight at the Carlyle. He'd just received a holiday bonus at work and was eager to spoil me in the form of a five-star hotel room. We spent hours listening to live jazz and knocking back dirty martinis at the hotel's famous Bemelmans Bar, which was dripping with holiday decorations. I might be Jewish, but I have to admit: there's something magical about Christmas in the city. It feels like *anything* can happen.

The next morning, Michael and I met some old G-III coworkers for breakfast. (Can you call a 1:00 p.m. meal breakfast?) I listened to them gossip about a potential merger, about the model who "forgot" to return the samples, about their upcoming trip to Paris Fashion Week…and I had the same powerful feeling I'd had the other night at Chelsea's. Yes. I was definitely jealous.

Back in our room, I packed my favorite pleather leggings back into my Longchamp tote and thought about how I'd never wear them in Wisconsin. Madison is the kind of place where people dress down. Unless you're at a frat party, in which case you wear as little as physically possible; clothes are for staying warm. And staying warm alone. A cheesehead's wardrobe is comprised of thermal socks, Ugg boots, and giant parkas. If I dressed how I wanted to dress, people would have thought I was crazy.

My Madison existence had only one lifeline—okay, two if you count casual sex—fashion blogs. There weren't many influencers at the time, except for OGs like Rumi Neely of Fashiontoast and Elin Kling of Style by Kling. Those girls were my idols. Elin's site taught me a lot about Scandinavian fashion and minimal dressing. Rumi showed me how to dress for maximum sex appeal. I spent so many hours on their blogs that they started to feel like my friends. It scratched such a different itch than reading a fashion magazine.

One night, I went home early and called Ashley on my bitterly cold walk back to the dorms. The warm beer I'd been drinking became truth serum, and I started talking her ear off about how I seemed to fit in better with girls I followed on the internet than with girls at my own school. "If you like fashion blogs so much, why don't you just start one?" she suggested, no doubt sick of listening to me complain.

I woke up the next morning with a crushing hangover but still managed to drag my ass to the library. The first thing I did was Google "how to start a fashion blog." I clicked on a link for Blogspot, which as a first step demanded a URL for my new site. I thought for a moment, then decided to call the thing *Speak of Chic*. Why? For no other reason than I liked the way that name sounded.

I had no idea what I was doing, but started posting right away. I didn't have a camera other than the one on my circa 2010 phone, so *Speak of Chic* had no photos. Just text. The blog tackled hard hitting topics like the groutfit (all gray outfit) and fishtail fixation (you can figure that one out for yourself). I didn't care if anyone read it and barely shared the link; this was just *my* attempt at connecting with the fashion industry while I was exiled in Wisconsin.

When Presidents' Day rolled around in February, I took the bus down to meet Michael in Chicago. I arrived early, wanting to spend a few hours getting ready for a romantic night out on the town. In the end Michael's flight was delayed—like most flights arriving at O'Hare at that time of year, apparently—and he missed all of our plans for Friday evening.

Unwilling to accept defeat, I decided to spend the night preparing our room for steamy romance. I wanted him to be *floored* when he opened the hotel room door. I lit candles, donned lingerie, and ordered room service champagne. When Michael finally arrived, tired and exasperated, the stage was set for what ended up being the perfect long weekend, which included a lingering dinner at triple-Michelin-starred Alinea, a frigid trip to Millennium Park, and a late-night visit to the top of the (then) Sears Tower.

As we held hands on snowy Michigan Avenue, out-of-date holiday lights glittering all around us, Michael asked if I ever thought about taking things to the next level—about defining the relationship. "Of course, I think about it all the time," I replied. I may have needed that first semester to explore college without a relationship, but I was game to stop seeing other people if he was.

I boarded the bus back to Madison on Monday in an exclusive relationship.

Michael and I wouldn't see each other again until March, when he flew me to Miami for the Ultra Music Festival. (It was a *very* early birthday present.) I realized as I was unpacking clothes that I hadn't worn all year—clothes that were about flair, not survival on the frozen tundra—that this was the first time in a long time that I felt really good. That I felt like the person I wanted to be.

"What about transferring?" Mike asked during our last break-fast at the hotel's buffet, noticing how unenthusiastic I was to re-turn to Madison. I considered the suggestion. Sure, Madison had been fun. I could honestly say I'd gone to College with a capital C. But was there anything else to learn from another three years drinking PBR in frat house basements? No. All that staying would do was delay the start of my real life.

I would only transfer, though, if it was for fashion school. There was no reason to go through all that hassle only to end up at another liberal arts institution—say, Sarah Lawrence or Fordham. The main issue was that fashion schools were unlikely to accept any of the general credits I'd accrued during my fresh-man year. If I was going to transfer to Parsons or the Fashion Institute of Technology (FIT), I was going to have to start from scratch. As a freshman. Again.

"Don't let that deter you." Mike yawned as he stretched on the linen sheets in our hotel room. "So it might take you an extra year to graduate. At least you'll be where you want to be, learning what you want to learn." I bit my lip, deep in thought. He really was making sense. (The fact that transferring to a school in New York City meant Michael and I could be together every day was also an obvious bonus.)

With Michael's help, I filled out the applications right then and there. Literally on the floor of our Miami hotel room, still wearing our neon outfits from the music festival. We didn't eat. We both missed our flights. But less than three weeks later, a fat envelope arrived in Madison that congratulated me for being accepted to FIT. Chelsea and I would be classmates. I was moving to NEW YORK CITY! It was *perfect*.

It felt like a smile had been stitched onto my face. I glowed with the news. I raced to the common room, where my roommates were watching a movie with the boys across the hall, and yelled. "Please don't freak out, but I've been accepted to FIT," I began. "I'm going to transfer."

Of course, I expected them to be sad. We were best friends! And now we would have to part—such sweet sorrow! The real problem was that the four of us had already signed a lease for next year's off-campus apartment. I knew it was an inconvenience, but assumed they would ultimately want me to follow my heart.

Instead, the girls were furious. They berated me for bailing on our living situation. They insisted they would never find another roommate in time. And then, just like that, they dropped me like a pair of Crocs. Not only would I be leaving Madison without any credits; I would also be leaving without any friends. (Unless you count my internet friends Elin and Rumi, who didn't even know I existed.) I had become so close with these girls, friends I thought I would have for a lifetime. To suddenly lose that as if I meant nothing to them, just because I was following my dreams, was devastating.

As expected, none of my credits transferred. (Apparently Psychology 101 and Pattern Making have nothing in common?) I had to start over, a first semester freshman once more. The worst part was, the tight course schedule meant I'd never be able to study abroad or take internships. If I wanted to graduate even relatively on time, I would have to focus on nothing but school.

Mine was an inconvenient choice. The transition wasn't easy. But, oh, was it worth it. I knew when I felt the burn of jealousy that I wanted something very deeply. When Chelsea and my other fashion friends talked about their life in the city, I realized I wouldn't be happy until I made it there myself. New York isn't the only place where people can succeed in my industry, but I needed to be surrounded by people as passionate about style as I was. I had taken another risk, one that would ultimately yield a high reward.

So I packed my bags and left State Street behind.

Better Alone Than in Bad Company

I was raised to trust my gut. And while I'm *very* good at this in my professional life, when it comes to matters of the heart... well, my heart can't always hear my gut. I *used* to think my life was incomplete unless I had a boyfriend. I'm not sure if my fear of being alone stemmed from my parents' divorce, or if it was just an unfortunate character trait. Whatever the reason, though, I hated being single so much that I would keep dating guys even when my instincts told me not to.

It took me a while, but at the tender age of twenty-seven I finally know it's better to be alone than in bad company.

I left the University of Wisconsin in May 2011. I remember calling my friend Chelsea as soon as my plane landed at LaGuardia, promising that we were going to have the best summer of our lives. Why? Because we had decided to move in together! In New York City!

Chelsea, of course, already had nine Manhattan months under her belt. She wore cool clothes and regularly dined at fancy restaurants like Minetta Tavern. She had glamorous roommates who either worked in fashion or were studying to. She dated men old enough to make Michael look like a fetus. In essence, Chelsea had a jump start on starting her adult life. Hitching myself to her wagon seemed like the fastest way for me to do the same.

Together we found a one-bedroom flex on West Eleventh Street. We shared the space with two of Chelsea's previous roommates and an elevator that worked less often than a cell phone in the Hamptons. It was tiny; it was old; but it was *ours*. What I loved most was the location—it was the only banged-up walk-up on a block full of brownstones. Once we finished moving, though, I found myself with a lot of free time. Too much free time. Everyone else had summer internships lined up, but there was nothing on my calendar until school started in September.

My instinct was to hang with Michael, who had recently landed a job at FourSquare (and his own apartment in Soho, on the corner of Grand and West Broadway, to boot). His new place was a beautiful lofted studio perched one floor above a favorite restaurant of ours, Felix, where we had enjoyed so many boozy brunches the previous summer.

Michael's new job didn't leave him with a ton of free time, but he seemed eager to share what little time he had with me. As the summer passed, our relationship fell into an easy routine. I met Michael at his Flatiron office every day after work. We'd stroll leisurely back to his apartment, me asking about his day, and then we'd change clothes for a night out in the city. I remember romantic tours of the Guggenheim, drinks at Employees Only in the West Village, and late nights partying at Piano's on the Lower East Side. We even attended the occasional Brooklyn warehouse party, where I saw people on designer drugs I'd never even heard of.

Whenever Michael had to work late, I would go out with Chelsea and her gaggle of FIT fashionista friends. Her group seemed so chic and cool—especially compared to me, the Wisconsin transplant. They wore designer clothes, knew all the promoters at Lavo, and had a rotating roster of finance guys footing the bills for their nights out. And so time went by.

Until one afternoon while I was at home watching *The Ellen DeGeneres Show*, as I was prone to do in the middle of the day, when my dad called with news. Somehow he'd convinced a friend of a friend to secure a last minute internship for me with EMM group, the nightlife company that owned Tenjune, CATCH, and the soon-to-be-opened SL. Basically, this company operated the hottest clubs in the city.

The offer was a surprise, and a compelling one at that. I had always loved event planning, as evidenced by my enthusiasm for throwing themed sorority mixers back at Wisconsin. I could host a great *party*. Event planning wasn't something I had ever considered as a career path, but why turn down a golden opportunity to try it out? Plus, I was in serious need of something other than daytime television to occupy my hours. I accepted the internship.

EMM Group threw me right into the thick of things. It was the complete opposite of my experience at G-III—not just because I had a desk instead of a closet, but also because I had real responsibilities. My first task was to plan DJ Cassidy's thirtieth birthday party on the *Intrepid*, a retired aircraft carrier permanently docked in the Hudson River. (If you want that full story, there's an episode on my podcast #WeHeardWhat about it.) Another night, I was tasked with walking Diddy into Tenjune, then making sure he and his crew had whatever they needed. The first time anyone lent me an Hervé Leger dress was the night I had to work the door of SL.

Of course, as with any internship, there was still bitch work. There was the time I stayed at the office until 4:00 a.m. stuffing envelopes. I was sent on constant coffee runs and even had to run bottle service a few times when we were particularly low on staff. But still, I loved the nightlife scene. The entire industry is about working hard and playing harder, a major mantra of mine to this day.

Not only did I enjoy this new job, but I also happened to be really freaking good at it. Sure, I saw the sunrise more often than I saw my own apartment. But I was the company's most requested intern. It felt good to be wanted, especially after spending a year in Madison feeling like a sore thumb.

I was thrilled with this new development in my life. Michael, however, was not.

A few weeks into my internship, the dynamic between us started to change. Of course, I still loved Michael. But I no longer needed him. I stopped picking him up from work every day. I took longer to respond to his texts than he wanted. He complained constantly—about my long hours, about my short dresses, about my new friends.

As much as I tried to pretend it wasn't happening, at some point in the summer of 2010, Michael stopped being the sweet boy who'd encouraged me to leave Wisconsin and became a jealous, insecure man. The more I tried to explain that he should be happy I was finding my own life in the city, the angrier he seemed.

Michael certainly supported my new life whenever I could score his friends a free table at SL, or if I offered to join him for a romp in the bathroom at Westway. But he hated that the power had shifted in our relationship. Michael had always been the one with connections and experience; I had been the vulnerable new kid in town—the company intern or the unhappy college freshman. Now that I had access, opportunities, and independence of my own, he seemed threatened. (Don't even get me started on how jealous he was when I started *WeWoreWhat*.)

Stupidly, I ignored my gut and kept plodding forth in our relationship. Michael, however, pulled back. He stopped taking me to new restaurants. He stopped calling me every night before bed. He stopped talking about our future. I thought about dumping him, but it never felt like the right time. And besides, I was still so new to the city. The thought of being without him terrified me.

When classes began in the fall, they came as a welcome distraction. My first month of FIT was pure bliss. For the first time, I was exactly where I needed to be. It was intoxicating. Another benefit? The start of the semester—and the end of my internship—also seemed to calm Michael down. We were back in our old roles, with me as the young student and him as my older paramour. (That alone should have been reason enough to run.)

Since I had roommates, the two of us mostly slept at Michael's place. I was happy to do it. Even if things were strained between us, sharing a tense bed with my boyfriend still seemed better than sharing seven hundred square feet with three other girls. (How many New York relationships are based on real estate, I wonder?)

Then, one day in early November, everything changed. I arrived at Michael's apartment that night just as he was getting back from the gym. In a gesture that reminded me of the beginning of our relationship, he had booked a table for us at the ever-trendy Nobu downtown. I couldn't wait to get all dressed up for a romantic date night we frankly needed. Or so I thought.

Michael asked if I could confirm the time of our reservation while he hopped in the shower. Like an idiot, he handed me his MacBook and left. I was in the process of logging onto OpenTable when I noticed the yellow AIM icon hopping up and down at the bottom of the screen. I knew I shouldn't invade his privacy, but something told me to click it. My gut told me, "*Do it, Danielle. Just do it.*"

I clicked.

The message was from a girl named Crystal. (I've changed a lot of names in this book, but not Crystal's. You literally can't make that shit up.)

Fortunately, or perhaps unfortunately, I already knew about this girl. She was the pretty young thing in all of Michael's old Facebook photos—the only female in his college group of friends. When I'd asked about her at the beginning of our relationship, Michael admitted that they had slept together a few times without it turning into anything serious. Crystal had moved to Los Angeles after graduation to pursue a career in acting, and they'd lost touch. Or so he claimed.

So you can imagine my surprise when I scrolled through their AIM history and discovered that they were *actually* talking every day. What had started as a casual catch-up a few weeks earlier had developed into a full-blown sexual relationship with cybersex. They explicitly detailed all the things they wished they could still do to each other. It got worse. Intermixed with all of their lewd messages was a series of notifications about closed video chats, after which Michael would always say something like, "That was great."

Their last rendezvous had occurred just a few minutes ago, while I was probably in the cab on my way over.

My heart sank. I was stunned. Sure, I knew things weren't great between us, but it seemed like we'd been on an upswing since I started school. Plus, Michael knew what an explosive issue infidelity was for me, given my family history. Would he really do this to me? *How* could he do this to me?

I confronted Michael as soon as he got out of the shower. He tried every way of talking himself out of trouble—claimed I'd misread the messages; pretended that cybersex wasn't cheating; insisted that this was *my* fault for going through his computer. And then, as a final blow, he blamed me. Apparently if I hadn't been so busy lately, he wouldn't have needed to seek affirmation elsewhere.

This made my blood boil. "No!" My voice was rising with hysteria. I started to shriek. "I'm not going to let you manipulate me! What you did *is* cheating. I'm not a fool."

Then I turned and ran out the door, sobbing uncontrollably. The silk blouse I had bought for our romantic dinner became streaked with tears. A relationship that had taken sixteen months to build took only two minutes to end.

So there I was, walking the streets of Soho, having just moved one thousand miles to be with this guy. (I had also moved for FIT, but at the moment our doomed relationship felt more compelling.) The whole situation was like a fucking Vanessa Carlton song, but without the happy ending.

As I crossed Houston Street en route back to my crowded apartment, I wondered how I had ever allowed myself to become so lost in a romantic relationship. Why hadn't I trusted my gut? Responded to the red flags?

I shook back my hair and made a promise: never again would I ignore my female intuition. The situation, however awful, taught me that if you suspect something's going on with your partner, it most likely is. Never again would I date someone who made me feel "less than." Never again would I stay in a bad relationship for fear of being single. I deserved to be in a supportive, respectful re- lationship. (Spoiler alert: This wasn't my last bad boyfriend, and it would take several more till I practiced what I preached).

I looked down and saw my phone was ringing. It was Michael. I screened the call and kept walking. Because it really is better to be alone than in bad company.

Follow Your Passion

It should come as no surprise that I'm a passionate person. I've always been a bit…over the top…when it comes to things I love. But it wasn't until I started *WeWoreWhat* that I learned what the word "passion" truly means. (I'm not talking about sex right now, people. I'm talking about my dream job.)

From the moment I launched my site, my veins surged with the excitement—with the thrill of connectivity. Not only had I found my purpose, but it was one I could share with the world.

To tell this story, we'll have to back up to the weeks before my first class at FIT. It was August of 2010, which, despite the relationship drama, remains one of the best and most formative summers of my life. I was so excited to finally become a New Yorker, to become a fashion student, to become an adult.

There was only one thing I had to do before school could start: pick a major. After my internship with EMM Group, I was more conflicted than ever about what path to follow. Should I major in design, an homage to the beloved sewing machine that my grandmother had given me not so long ago? Should I study to become a buyer and help stores decide what items to stock? Or did I want to focus on event planning, building upon everything I learned this summer?

In the end, I chose to major in advertising, marketing, and communications (AMC). To my family, who had assumed I'd pursue something creative, this was as shocking as *La La Land* losing the Oscar. But AMC had the most well-rounded classes, where I could learn about both creative and business. (Think: Integrated Marketing Communications, Publicity Workshop, Fashion Business Practices.) But I didn't care if the coursework thrilled me; I only cared that I could study fashion and graduate four years later as an employable New York woman.

When the first day of school *finally* rolled around—I had been waiting for so long!—I arrived feeling confident. I wore the cool girl outfit that had taken me an entire week to put together, mixing vintage trousers (thrifted from a store called Beacon's Closet) with an oversized white button-down (stolen from my dad's closet) and black loafers (old, but worn to casual perfection). The final effect? Low-key chic.

Unfortunately, said confidence only lasted about as long as my first attempt at sexual intercourse…because everyone *else* at the school looked like they had arrived fresh from Art Basel. The students, the teachers—hell, even the office administrators— were already wearing next season's haul. My Aldos drowned in a sea of Gucci loafers. I had spent time on the FIT campus before when I took that sewing class back in high school, but I didn't remember people dressing like this. The full-time students I encountered now were serious about fashion in a way that I'd never seen.

Every day on FIT's campus was like a trip to the Metropolitan Museum of Art's annual costume exhibit. (Okay, maybe that's a *bit* of a stretch. But you get the point.) My classmates made daring fashion choices. They saw style as a fun means of self-expression. I remember the first time I heard someone say they were wearing an outfit "ironically."

I thought about all my high school friends who were in other states for college. I thought about girls around the world who loved fashion, but weren't lucky enough to be surrounded by it every day. If only there was a way for them to see the outfits that were now inspiring me on a daily basis.

That's when the light bulb went off. There *was* a way to share what I was seeing. And I knew just how to do it.

The next morning, I rode the subway to Penn Station. Most New Yorkers avoid midtown like the plague. It's loud, it smells, and it's mobbed with tourists who still think it's the center of the city. That day, however, I traveled into the belly of the beast on a larger quest. Where was I headed? To B&H, the legendary photography store on the corner of Thirty-Fourth Street and Ninth Avenue. It's stood there since 1973, as much a New York institution as the Empire State Building or our cat-sized-rat population.

I pushed open the glass door and marched toward the first employee I saw—a young, pimply guy about my age. I wasn't entirely convinced he knew more about photo equipment than his older colleagues, but I could tell from the way he was staring that he was going to be willing to spend some serious time helping me out.

No matter how hard I try, I cannot remember that B&H employee's name. But I owe him a lot, because that guy sold me my first camera a Canon DSLR point and shoot. He generously spent two hours teaching me how to use the thing. When I left B&H later that day, I was in love. (Not with the sales associate, obviously. With the camera.)

Back in my apartment that evening, I pored over the camera's handbook as if my life depended on it. Then I called my roommates into my room and asked if they would be my practice models. My goal that night was to learn how to take the perfect candid photo. I wanted the subject precisely in focus, but the background behind her to be blurred. (The basic rule here is the wider your aperture or the lower your f-number is, the shallower the depth of field). After a dozen or so retakes, I finally got it.

From that day forward, I possessed a revised sense of purpose: to photograph the best looks around FIT's campus, a.k.a. street style. I did it for myself—to remember the girl who insisted fanny packs were coming back, the boy who always had a perfectly tilted beret. But I also did it for my friends who weren't surrounded by the city style I saw daily. Getting dressed should be the easiest part of your day, and I wanted to help make sure it was—whether you lived in a big city or not.

Once I catalogued all the inspiration, I figured, why not share it with friends across the country? Didn't everyone want to know how the most creative New Yorkers were putting everyday looks together? Or where the chicest woman you've ever seen bought her vintage bag? Didn't we all want the insights, encouragement, and a template for a kick-ass look?

In retrospect, I'd decided to become a street style photographer—not that I even knew that word at the time.

My new routine went like this: I would walk around FIT until I found a target—someone whose outfit was so perfect or unusual that it begged to be photographed. Then I would approach and ask to snap a photo. If they agreed, which most did, I would whip out my tape recorder (also courtesy of B&H) and asked a few questions about their look. *Where did you buy those booties? Is that scarf vintage Chanel? Who was your inspiration for this outfit?*

Soon word spread around campus that newcomer Danielle was photographing girls for a secret project. My classmates were excited to be a part of it. They started going out of their way to casually pass *me*, as if my camera's click was some sort of stamp of approval. (I like to think that me not taking someone's picture was as devastating as walking past famed street style photographer Bill Cunningham without warranting a second glance. But it probably wasn't.)

What I needed now was a way to share my photos. Hence my return to Blogspot, the same platform that had hosted my previous blog, *Speak of Chic*, the year before. Blogspot had dozens of customizable themes that would allow my website to be up and running (and beautiful) in just a few hours. The only issue? You have to pick a URL before doing anything else. For some reason I'll never quite understand, my fingers entered WeWoreWhat.com as if they already knew what to type.

We, because: We, the girls of New York City.

Wore, because: It's what we wore that day.

What, because: I would detail every aspect of their ensembles.

Phew. The URL was available.

I began uploading photos that very day, along with whatever details I had scrounged about the subjects' outfits (e.g., "jeans, Rag & Bone, circa 2008"). Each post was blasted in a mass email to everyone I'd ever met—friends from high school and even co-workers from my past internships. No email in my address book was left unturned.

I didn't know if anyone was actually opening my emails until I started to receive messages from friends and friends of friends. "I love this particular item—where can I get it?" "If that piece is un-available, where can I get something similar?" "Is there a cheaper place to buy that?" I spent hours researching how to replicate looks for less, scouring the internet for the perfect Steve Madden version of those Prada mules.

I couldn't believe how many readers my new blog already had—all from word of mouth. Truth be told, I never thought about what would happen if *WeWoreWhat* took off. Blogs taking off wasn't a thing people even talked about at the time. When I started the site, I honestly didn't care if I had five readers or five thousand. I was just having fun doing something that inspired me, and that's why it resonated with people.

Soon I began traveling to different parts of the city to pho-tograph fashion beyond the confines of FIT's campus. When February Fashion Week rolled around in 2011, I decided to stand outside the shows and photograph It Girls as they paraded inside. Of course, I wasn't going to run up to the likes of Chloe Sevigny and interview her about her outfit. But I could reverse engineer her looks by finding similar (and more affordable) items online.

This was back when New York Fashion Week took place at Lincoln Center on the Upper West Side. I'll never forget the blus-tery day I was sitting on the edge of the giant fountain that sits out front of the arts complex, scrolling through my B&H-bought DSLR to review everyone who had just walked into the Marc Jacobs show.

That's when I heard someone speak.

"Miss? Can I take your photo?"

I looked up and saw an eager photographer, his camera pointed in my direction.

"Of me?" I asked, disbelieving.

"You're Danielle Bernstein, aren't you?"

And then everything changed.

Stay Ahead of the Curve

I sprinted back to my Greenwich Village apartment. What was the rush? I needed to be at my computer the *second* that photographer posted the picture of me at Lincoln Center. I wondered who he worked for. Maybe *Vogue*? Or ELLE.com?

"Chelsea!" I yelled, hoping my friend was around. "You won't believe what just happened to me." But there was no response. She wasn't home. Our resident cockroaches could share my excitement.

I scoured the internet every few hours but never found my photo. Even so, that single snap changed everything for me.

I started to think. Was it possible that my style had developed so much that it could be inspiring all on its own? Not only had I learned a lot from starting my blog, but simply being in Manhattan had had an impact on me. Over the past few months,

I had learned how to thrift, how to pair pieces in a sophisticated way, how to pick silhouettes that were flattering on my body. I had returned to the way I'd thought about clothes during those teenage shopping trips to Century 21 and Macy's. I also felt way more comfortable experimenting with fashion here in New York than I did in Madison or even back home on Long Island. Had all these experiences combined to make my own looks become blog worthy?

I have always loved attention, but used to hate being in front of the camera. While my brothers were the hams, I became insecure when the lens turned in my direction. The scrutiny made me feel vulnerable. During family portraits, I tried to edge behind the group and stay in the background—more like an art director than a model. ("Alec, can you stand up straighter and unclench that hand on Mom's shoulder?")

My followers may find this hard to believe, but I'm *still* a little uncomfortable having my picture taken. That's why I was always wearing sunglasses in early photos on *WeWoreWhat*. I claimed the reason for the eyewear was to keep the focus on the clothes, but really the eyewear just let me hide. They were my personal safety blanket.

My then-apartment was decidedly unbloggable. Two of my roommates had covered every damn wall with that one *Gossip Girl* poster of Serena and Blaire eating ice cream that everyone seemed to have at the time. Therefore, I decided to take my photo shoots to the streets and make Manhattan my studio. I enlisted my roommate and fellow FIT student Jess as my first photographer. (Something she did for free, thank God, because I could barely afford Pinkberry toppings back then, let alone an employee.)

Jess is a loud girl of Italian descent. The two of us shared a love of urban style and general rowdiness. We were a lot alike, and she's still one of my best friends to this day. I remember her parents weren't helping her pay for FIT, so she was always working multiple jobs. I admired her independence, her aura of maturity, her hustle.

Together we spent days combing the city, making a list of all the best places to shoot. The ultimate finds were solid brick walls, which I quickly came to realize made the best backgrounds. Only once Jess and I found that *perfect* spot, would I pose, working my angles as I tried not to inhale subway steam or embarrass myself in front of the tourists who often gathered, assuming I was someone famous. I pranced back and forth across the street until we got the perfect "candid" shot.

Sure, I was out of my comfort zone. But I was loving every second of it.

So what happened when I posted those first photos of myself on *WeWoreWhat*? My readers took notice in a big way. They loved this new spin on the blog, which put my personal style front and center. People had been following me for months without knowing who I was, and now the woman behind the camera had been revealed. The moment I changed from street style to personal style was the moment that paved my future success.

Featuring my own clothes also meant I could offer more service-oriented content. I could dive deeper into the thought process behind each look since I was the one who had put it together. No longer was my blog just helpful eye candy; now I could actually walk readers through an outfit's step-by-step creation. I could explain why I paired that blazer with those jeans, why a certain pair of boots' shaft height was important because it cut my leg in the right place. I started offering more practical help, linking to the best skinny jeans on the market right now or the perfect white T-shirts. I helped readers find silhouettes that worked with different body types, how to mix loose and tight. As the blog evolved, my purpose came into focus: to help women everywhere get dressed in the morning. It wasn't just a hobby anymore. It was a mission.

Soon it became obvious that my style was resonating more with my readers than street style. It got more views, more comments, more attention. After a few weeks, I decided to stop posting street style entirely and only post my own outfits.

But to do that I had to up my photography game. My photos needed to look more professional, which meant I had to learn how to edit. Not wanting to spring for Photoshop, which is actually a really expensive platform, I sought out free photo editing web-sites. My favorite was PicMonkey—the ultimate tool to smooth out a wrinkle here or remove garbage off the street there. (Now, of course, there are a million apps for this).

Slowly but surely, my blog started to grow as I continued to showcase my own style. I ached to dedicate more time to it, but was struggling to balance *WeWoreWhat* with my rigorous coursework at FIT and a new internship I had just accepted for the fall semester. (So much for not overloading my schedule so I could graduate on time.) Add in any sort of normal social life, and I was drowning in commitments. I've never been the person who needs a lot of sleep, but in those days, I was lucky to get four hours. It was a grind.

I started my internship at NowManifest, a curated platform that consolidated leading fashion blogs in one place—kind of like an early version of the Instagram news feed. Interning there meant I began working with and befriending some of the world's first big bloggers, like Bryan Grey Yambao (BryanBoy), Rumi Neely (Fashiontoast), and Elin Kling (Style by Kling)—people whose style I had worshipped ever since I discovered their blogs while living in Wisconsin.

I worked tirelessly to endear myself to those influencers, spending late nights writing blog posts for them or bringing their favorite lunches to the office. No gesture was too big or too small. I went the extra mile whenever possible, and eventually they started inviting me to events. I will *never* forget the first time Elin asked me to go out with her. We attended the H&M x Versace fashion show. Being a guest—instead of the one checking the guest list—made me feel like I'd crossed to the other side.

I have always been a fearless networker. So when Elin brought me somewhere as her plus one, I was able to speak to people like Nina Garcia (the editor and chief of *ELLE*, whom I now consider a friend), without fright. Even at star-studded fashion shows, there was never anyone too big or too powerful for me to approach. I could always march up and introduce myself with a firm handshake. And then, if the conversation went well, I would ask for that person's card or email to stay in touch.

Soon I learned to research who was going to be at which party in advance. That way I could come prepared with conversation topics. ("No way, you also grew up on Long Island? What an unexpected coincidence!") There's nothing like a personal connection to make someone want to help you.

The coolest thing about my internship was that NowManifest happened to sell to Fairchild Fashion Media (then a subsidiary of Condé Nast, which owned my favorite publications, such as *Women's Wear Daily*) while I was still working there. As the youngest person on the team, my colleagues assumed—accurately—that I must be really "good at the internet." And it was for that reason that they put me in charge of onboarding our two newest bloggers who had come courtesy of our new partnership with Conde: Derek Blasberg and Anna Dello Russo.

Onboarding a blogger meant teaching them how to use our preferred content management platform (WordPress) so that they could start blogging on NowManifest. For Anna, who was born in Italy and is now editor-at-large for *Vogue Japan*, I was mostly responsible for correcting the grammar of her nonnative English. For Blasberg, on the other hand, I had to spend more than a few late nights at Mercer Kitchen teaching him how to operate the backend of WordPress. Not every fashion creative was an internet whiz back then.

The more time I dedicated to NowManifest, the harder it was to balance all the commitments in my life. I was almost happy Michael had cybercheated on me and broke my heart. (The key word being *almost*.) My single status did, however, provide more free hours to focus on my *true* love: the fashion industry.

My boss was impressed enough by my hard work at NowManifest and my own site's content that he entered me in a Refinery29 competition called the Next Big Style Blogger. Contestants were asked to perform a series of tasks, such as styling the same shirt three different ways and putting an outfit together for less than $100. I pulled several all-nighters and skipped a week's worth of FIT classes in order to finish my application on time. And, let me tell you, it was worth it, because…

I won.

My prize was a partnership with Bar III, one of Macy's in-house brands. (They make ready-to-wear dresses, pants—nothing too fancy.) I couldn't believe that my first collaboration was going to be with one of the biggest department stores in the world. Somewhere I actually shopped for my own clothes! And the news got better: Macy's wanted to pair me with an already established blogger with whom I would spend the summer touring America and running Bar III pop-ups in Macy's across the country.

The other girl just so happened to be Aimee Song from *Song of Style*, who had a much larger following and was someone I had admired for many months. In the span of one year, I had not only met, but also started working with the biggest names in the blogger game—the very same people who had inspired me to launch *WeWoreWhat*. What a wonderful way to start my twentieth year on this planet.

Aimee was only four years older than me but was already a giant in the burgeoning blog community. She was beautiful, had great style, and knew the industry inside and out—but that's not what impressed me. What really stood out about Aimee, both in person and in her posts, was how seamlessly she was able to integrate brand partnerships into her content. She was one of the first to monetize her blog and taught me to think of myself as a potential asset for advertisers.

Unlike Aimee, I didn't have a big enough following to pursue paid brand partnerships. All I could hope for at the time was to pull a few pieces to style, photograph, and then return. I wasn't paying them, and they weren't paying me. Borrowing clothes, however, meant I always had new outfits to post on my blog. (I also visited my favorite thrift store, Buffalo Exchange, on a weekly basis to keep my closet fresh.)

I don't know if it was Aimee's support, the Macy's partnership, or all the publicity I got from Refinery29, but *WeWoreWhat*'s following started growing like wildfire after that summer. Previously, I had been lucky to add a few hundred new followers each week. Now I was attracting thousands. Was it possible that blogging, which I had only ever considered a passion project, might actually become a career? As it was for Elin, Rumi, and Aimee?

Another thing I learned that year was that data would be my greatest asset. I taught myself how to track the number of impressions and views on every post using Google Analytics. I created custom bit.ly links that tracked click-throughs to prove the extent of my reach. Whenever I worked with a clothing company, even if it was unpaid, I would call the brand manager to record how many sales my content had generated. Then I presented those numbers *back* to the same brand as proof for future compensation, and that's how I started earning income through *WeWoreWhat*.

At one point during 2012, I downloaded a new app called Instagram. I definitely wasn't one of the first people on it. Instagram had been around for more than a minute before I made my first post: a blurry picture of my birthday cake. It took months for me to realize there could be synergy between my blog and this new social media platform. At first all I wanted to post were snaps of house parties and nights out with friends.

Until one night when Jess invited me to the birthday party of one of her coworkers at Hotel Chantelle on the Lower East Side. The venue has since lost its cachet, but back then, it was *the* place to be. Everyone wanted to party there—finance bros, students, and, yes, burgeoning bloggers. We were all jostling for a table on the rooftop, which had been decorated to feel like a park. There was dangly greenery, functioning Parisian lampposts, and a killer view of the city.

Jess and I happened to show up in identical outfits—a little black dress with biker boots. We laughed and each posted a photo of us to Instagram with the hashtag #twinning.

"Holy shit," Jess yelled a few minutes later, her voice already hoarse from screaming over the music. "Your post already has so many likes."

"Is that not normal?" I asked between sips of tequila on the rocks.

"Fuck no. Look!" she replied.

My post had garnered four hundred likes and sixteen comments in less than thirty minutes. (For comparison, Jess's version of the same photo only had ten likes and no comments.) I didn't even know half of the people engaging with me. They were dying to know where they could buy my dress, how they could copy my hair. At that moment my alcohol-addled brain had a breakthrough: maybe Instagram had business potential.

But you have to remember: this was 2012. Instagram was still in its nascent phase. Only two years old, no one knew what the thing was. Was it more like LinkedIn or Facebook? Or was it a picture version of Twitter? No one knew, and therefore the platform was a freaking free-for-all.

Still, it was dawning on me that the tool could be a major asset to my blog. Why not post my blog photos to my Instagram as a way to direct those followers to my site? Instagram was on our phones; our phones were always in our hands. Duh. This was the fastest way to reach people.

No longer would my readers have to open a web browser to visit the world of *WeWoreWhat*. Now I was in their pockets, with them all the time. At the tips of their fingers. In theory, Instagram played off people's obsession with reality TV, letting followers see what bloggers were actually wearing while we were still wearing it—even before Instagram Stories. Now I could post in real time. Gone were the days of running home to plug my camera into my computer. Instagram was instant, mobile, perfect.

In retrospect, I may have been one of the first bloggers to consciously cultivate my Instagram following and prioritize that over my blog's readership. The rules to growing my following were simple. I engaged with my audience—whenever someone commented, I wrote back. I used hashtags to make myself more discoverable. I created a content calendar to plan my posts in advance. I also alternated between different types of photos—an outfit of the day post was followed by a new product arrival or lunch location—so that my feed never got stale.

After Instagram enabled tagging in 2013, my following grew astronomically. Now when I posted an outfit, I could tag every brand that I was wearing—and then that company would tag me in return, introducing me to their followers. I like to call this *double exposure*, and it's the ultimate way to get eyeballs on your page. Always, always, always tag everyone and everything you can (and ask them to return the favor). And if a magazine like *Harper's Bazaar* wants to use my photo, they have to tag my account.

If you look at the strategic decisions I made during the early years of my blog—going from street style photos to pictures of myself, focusing so much on Instagram instead of the blog—it seems like I had a plan. In reality, I was flying by the seat of my pants, paving my path in an industry that was still mostly undefined. Hell, I was helping to pave the industry.

I actually think one of the biggest reasons I was successful was *because* I remained so nimble. I paid close attention to what both readers and the market were demanding. If something seemed to resonate with my readers, I gave them more of it. If the industry asked for something, I leaned into it. That's why *We Wore What* will always be a work in progress, and why I'm always asking for feedback. We need to be ready to change day by day. Embracing that is why my blog succeeded where so many others failed.

Take the Plunge

It wasn't until the end of 2012 that I started dedicating more time to my Instagram than my blog. Because at some point during my weeks off FIT, my follow count hit two hundred thousand. WeWoreWhat.com, for comparison, averaged one hundred fifty thousand unique visitors per month. It didn't take a rocket scientist to see more people were engaging with me on social media than on the World Wide Web.

Continuing to grow my social media presence, however, took more time than I expected. I was still doing the work but had begun to slack at FIT. I might have slept through a lecture because I'd stayed up the entire previous night editing a post, but at least I was there. When I left campus at the end of the day, I made a vague attempt to study (although I usually got bored within an hour and took to the street for blog photos). It wasn't a conscious choice, but

I was naturally beginning to prioritize things that would benefit *WeWoreWhat* over my schoolwork.

But by the spring semester of 2013—when I was running not only a blog, but also a popular Instagram feed—I started to skip most of my classes. I stayed at home to plan my content calendar. Days were spent meeting with brands and going to press previews and nights networking at industry events. I'll never forget the one time I actually did show up to my Online Integrated Marketing class, only to realize that I knew more about the topic than the professor. (I have always been a firm believer in learning by doing.)

Emails poured into my inbox from angry teachers demanding an explanation for my many absences. But it wasn't until I skipped a Publicity Workshop final exam at the end of the semester (to attend a brand's launch event) that the head of my program called me into his office.

Professor Romano and I had gotten close during my time at FIT. He was supercool—a father figure of sorts. Professor Romano was one of the first people to believe that *WeWoreWhat* could actually be something more than a hobby. We would hang out between classes and work together on making my schedule flexible enough so I could focus on blogging. (These days, I still guest lecture in his classes on a regular basis.)

"I've tried to support you, but we need to discuss what's happening," he said one day over takeout coffee in his office. "Your report card has nothing but incompletes."

Mr. Romano suggested that I try taking some online courses over the summer. Not only would the remote nature give me additional time to focus on *WeWoreWhat*, but it would also get credits out of the way for a lighter fall semester. I had to admit, it sounded like a pretty good plan.

Of course, I never finished a single online class and was therefore called back to Mr. Romano's office. This time he was full of questions: "Why do you even want to attend FIT? Should you really return for the fall semester? Should you take some time off? Spend the next few months on your blog and then come back in the spring if you want?"

The guy had a point. It was ludicrous to pay tuition for classes that I wasn't even attending. I became obsessed with the story of Michael Kors, a FIT legend who dropped out in the 1970s to pursue his designs. Of course, Mr. Kors has gone on to become one of the biggest names in fashion—and maybe I could too? Was the half-assed pursuit of a college degree only holding me back instead of helping me?

A decision had to be made: Should I risk dropping out of the college I had recently transferred to and upend my life for a second time in two years? Should I forsake it all to chase a dream?

I may have grown up comfortably in the middle class, but there was no trust fund for me to dip into when times were tough. No wealthy aunt to benevolently float my bills. So if I was going to leave school and try to make it on my own as a young blogger... well, there were going to be some serious changes to my lifestyle.

Immediately after making the decision to leave FIT come fall, I went out and found two jobs. The first was at a clothing company called Reformation. I spent much of 2013 on the floor at their Soho location, serving double duty as both a sales associate and a store merchandiser. (Merchandisers help brands dress mannequins, decide what product to put on what rack, etc.) I also worked part time at another clothing brand called Necessary Clothing, helping them style shoots for their ecommerce website. I chose the jobs because they not only supplied me with a paycheck and flexible hours, but also access to more clothes I could feature on my blog.

I realize that most people would consider two retail jobs more of a time commitment than college. But it really was more manageable—I was able to create my own schedule on a week-to-week basis. I had amazing coworkers who were always happy to trade shifts. Plus, I needed the "proof of responsibility" if I was going to get through the next step in my post-FIT plan—telling my parents that I might need some financial support while I got *WeWoreWhat* up and running.

My father is the parent my brothers and I go to for career advice—the one I needed in my corner if this plan was going to work. But convincing Glenn Bernstein that he should support his only daughter during a "leave of absence" from college was going to be a challenge. Especially when both of my siblings were spending their college years studying in the hallowed halls of the University of Michigan's Ross School of Business.

It was time to pull out the big guns.

Assuming I was more likely to be taken seriously in an office setting than at the Capital Grille, the steakhouse where my dad and I liked to spend time together, I emailed his assistant to set a meeting at his Fifth Avenue building. (Considering how much I hate midtown, the venue was supposed to signal I meant business.) I even donned my favorite gray Topshop pantsuit for the occasion, a groutfit that would have made *Speak of Chic* proud.

My hands were shaking with nerves. I settled into a plush leather chair in the all-glass conference room, waiting for my dad to arrive. I reminded myself that like any good entrepreneur, I had come ready with a formal PowerPoint presentation that laid out my proposal. (I had seen enough episodes of *Shark Tank* to bring a well-thought-out plan for both my business and my life.)

The pitch was simple: I would take a semester off school to pursue *WeWoreWhat* full time. The blog was starting to monetize, and I needed more time to focus if I wanted to maintain that upward trajectory. If I couldn't fully support myself by December, then I would give up *WeWoreWhat* and return to FIT with my Fendi tail between my legs. And if I could…well, I would never look back.

"And how exactly do you plan to pay your bills during this break, Danielle?" my dad asked, his hands calmly folded on the conference table.

I explained that in addition to the money I was starting to make through *WeWoreWhat*, I had also found two part-time jobs.

I walked him through my new budget and explained that if he paid my rent, I could take care of all other expenses. Every one of my dad's questions were answered, but somehow he still had more:

What's Instagram?

How does anyone make money off a social media platform?

Are you going to spend the time creating content or meeting with the brands?

And, most important, what makes you think you can be successful when no one has ever done this before?

Sensing the conversation wasn't going my way, I reached for my ace in the hole: an Excel spreadsheet that I had prepared to show what other bloggers and myself were charging advertisers per CPM. (CPM is an important marketing term that determines cost per thousand impressions. An impression is just a fancy word for views.) I knew what I could charge with my current following of over two hundred thousand, and also projected what I would be able to make as that number grew.

In the end, my dad was supportive. I'll never forget the look on his face when it finally clicked for him. "I don't necessarily understand what you're doing, but I trust you and want to see where you can take it."

My adrenaline surged, and my pulse went a million miles a minute. I broke my professionalism and threw my arms around my father, thanking him profusely for the opportunity to risk everything and chase my dreams. It meant so much that he trusted me enough to help. I had honestly expected him to tell me to stay in school. Neither of us could have known that my follower account would skyrocket so much in the next three months that I would no longer need rent money.

I don't want to encourage people to drop out of school. There's a lot to be said for a college education. I, for one, loved my time at FIT and continue to speak on panels there to this day. I'm still hoping Mr. Romano will come through with his promise of an honorary degree (hint hint).

I do want people to know that living in New York City when you're menially employed and trying to launch a business is *tough*. It's one of the most expensive cities in the world. I can't express how many times I hauled trash bags full of clothing to Buffalo Exchange so that I could sell them and (hopefully) make enough money to eat something other than ramen that week.

As for me, I had a plan. And, perhaps more important, I knew how to communicate it. I was also fortunate enough to have a parent who heard me out, who believed in me enough to offer financial support. Without his encouragement…well, I don't know where I would be.

What I do want is to urge people to take risks and follow their dreams. Because unless the goal is to be a doctor or a lawyer—a job where there are clear, predetermined steps—there's no cookie-cutter path to success. I want to be clear that I do not suggest or promote dropping out of college. My path took me in a different direction, and it was a different time back then. Sometimes you just have to trust your gut and take the plunge. I can only speak for myself, but it was the smartest thing I ever did.

Don't Be Afraid to Get Help

Anyone scrolling through the speed dial section of my iPhone will see that the most important people in my life are: Maureen (Moe) Paretti, my parents, and the person I'm dating. In that exact order. (Of course, the Ear Inn also ranks pretty high, based on the fact that this Soho restaurant delivers me a lunchtime kale Caesar salad with grilled salmon on top almost every day.)

But the point is, that no matter what else changes, Moe always comes first. Always.

Moe started as one of *We Wore What*'s first interns back in 2013. Since then, she has worked her way up the chain and now serves as the chief operating officer for the entire company. What that actually means, beyond Moe's status as my emotional support human and general right hand gal, changes by the second. Her ability to adapt and learn new skills based on whatever I need at a particular moment is one of Moe's best attributes.

But in order for you to truly understand just how much of a unicorn Moe really is, you first need to hear how we met.

My blog took off after I left FIT and was able to focus my attention on it. My Instagram started attracting thousands of new followers each week. And while the high-speed growth was certainly exciting—and meant that brands were starting to take me more seriously—it meant there was more work to be done than I could handle on my own.

I decided to hire an intern. At first, I found friends and friends of friends to help out whenever the workflow demanded it. Each girl was nice and hardworking, but there was always something missing. Most of the interns could complete a task when I delegated it to them, but weren't proactive enough to anticipate my needs. They weren't my person.

If I was going to bring someone on more long term and actually commit to training them, then they would need to have that "your brain is an extension of my brain" factor that's so important with those first few hires at a new company. Early stage employees should be champions of the brand, ultimately helping to chart the business's trajectory. It's okay to be picky.

Then, out of the blue, I got an email: "Hi! My name is Maureen Paretti, but I go by Moe. I am going into my sophomore year at FIT this fall. I have recently become interested in fashion bloggers through their websites and Instagrams. I came across yours, and

I am in love with it! I don't want to be a blogger myself, but I am intrigued by how you make money." The email went on from there. It was heartfelt, honest, and to the point.

So, naturally, I ignored it.

In typical Danielle fashion, the email disappeared into the ever-expanding abyss that is my inbox. I wouldn't remember to respond to it until New York Fashion Week came around and it became clear from the number of shows missed and samples lost that I needed help. Fast.

Unfortunately, Moe had already accepted an internship at some prestigious fashion house called Halston or whatever. NBD. And since she was a student at FIT, there wasn't time to fit in both positions.

The good news is that after just two weeks of delivering $10,000 dress samples and making coffee runs, Moe realized she wasn't built for the typical fashion internship. (She must not have read my chapter about bitch work.) She reached back out to me, saying she wanted to intern somewhere she could be involved and have more responsibility. Could *WeWoreWhat* be that place?

We decided to meet the next day at a Coffee Bean on the corner of Bleecker and Sullivan.

I'll never forget the first time I saw her. I walked into the coffee shop to find a petite redhead already waiting at a table. She was wearing a Zara romper that looked more like pajamas than clothes (cool), a slicked back ponytail (cooler), a nose ring (even cooler) and edgy biker boots (the coolest). I don't believe in love at first sight when it comes to romantic relationships, but I do believe in it when it came to Moe.

I marched over and, without sitting down, asked the only thing I needed to know from Moe at the time: "Are you going to kill me?"

"Not today," she said with a cheerful smile. That's when I knew she was for me.

Moe and I left the Coffee Bean after chatting and walked back to my apartment. We were ready to jump into things that very same day.

WeWoreWhat had a big enough following to start monetizing, but it's not as if brand partnerships were pouring in on a daily basis. (My calendar didn't get totally crazy until later that year.) The only tasks I had for Moe some days were to steam clothes and run around town picking up, you guessed it, samples. (I'll bet she questioned her choice to quit Halston for me on more than one occasion.) Meanwhile I would stay at home reaching out to brands about potential partnerships and doing research for our next team shopping trip. (I was constantly reinvesting my income into more clothes so that I always had something new to photograph.)

Although my life looked glamorous on Instagram, the truth is Moe and I spent most of our time in yoga pants. We watched a *lot* of daytime television in my apartment, planning our entire day around *The Ellen DeGeneres Show* and *Bethenny*. (RIP to the latter.) I can still hear myself saying "Stop steaming, Moe. It's time for our three o'clock."

Since you can't watch TV without snacks, Moe and I developed a close relationship with the men at the deli beneath my apartment, and they knew our order by heart. I always got a chicken cutlet wrap, which I chased with a coffee (almond milk and one sugar, please). Moe paired her turkey and mayo wrap with green tea. (Of course, we would never eat that stuff today. Moe is a vegan, and I'm unable to eat anything fried without feeling like complete shit after.)

Moe and I would haul our deli wraps upstairs, then watch TV as we lay on my white leather couch (which was actually small enough to be considered a love seat). Our feet often touched in the middle. We were like a modern version of the Willy Wonka grandparents, but with nicer clothes and slicker ponytails.

Looking back, it's hard to remember there was ever a time when Moe and I had that little to do. Sure, we had busy days, but the workload was inconsistent. When we weren't watching daytime television, you could most likely catch us preplanning outfits—five outfits, one for every day of the week. Then we'd hire a photographer and have him shoot the entire next weeks' worth of posts in a single go. (It's incredibly important for burgeoning influencers to post consistently, and I was always worried about having enough content to meet my once-a-day posting quota.)

What's craziest to me is that I ever had the time to plan a week's worth of outfits in advance. These days, I always post in real time. I get dressed in the morning (usually posting the outfit's creation on InstaStories), then ask whoever happens to be with me if they can snap a cool shot of what I'm wearing on my phone. It's like a Danielle Bernstein reality show that you can watch every night after work to see what I wore and where I went that day.

But I need to stop thinking about Instagram before Stories, because that was a dark time…

Since we didn't have *that* much to do, it didn't really matter what time Moe and I started work in the morning. We got in the habit of going out every night, becoming regulars at all the cool spots in Lower Manhattan. We'd go to ACME and flirt with bankers blowing off steam during the two hours before they had to go back to work in the morning. We'd go to Paul's Baby Grand and flirt with the bartenders paying their way through art school.

Since *WeWoreWhat* paid Moe a small stipend, but not enough to live on, I even helped her get a hostess gig at a downtown club called Gilded Lily on West Fifteenth Street. In its glory days, the club was one of the last truly great openings in the Meatpacking District. It was a gold-bedazzled underground bunker of a club. How Moe was able to balance her job there with FIT classes and her internship…I'll never know.

The scales seemed to tip around the time I hit five hundred thousand followers on Instagram. It wasn't until one million followers that I could truly call myself a *macro-influencer*, but five hundred thousand was still very significant. For the first time I was making enough money to breathe. The good news was that I could finally afford my own apartment. The bad news was that downtime disappeared. Moe and I were forced to eat our wraps in Ubers while darting between meetings from Midtown to Soho and all around the city.

I also signed with an agent named Jen Powell following an introduction by her client Chiara Ferragni, one of the most influential bloggers in the world. After a single meeting at Soho House, single-mother-turned-dealmaker Jen managed to whisk away any concerns about signing over 20 percent of every paycheck. Because unlike other agents—who mostly negotiate incoming deals, which *is* important—Jen was focused on generating new business. She was a down-and-dirty hustler who understood things like "usage rights" and also repped the biggest names in the business. She actually created what was known as the "talent division" at modeling agencies, which represented a fresh, nontraditional group of people. Naturally, I signed with her.

In an effort to keep up with the avalanche of incoming work, Moe moved as many of her classes online as possible. The ones she couldn't, she jammed into two days a week. Moe was in, dedicating every hour possible to *WeWoreWhat*. I started to experience déjà vu, flashing back to my own experience trying to survive fashion school while building the business. Clearly Moe was the only person who cared about *WWW* as much as I did.

As is natural with anyone making such a large sacrifice, Moe started to demand more autonomy—she wanted to be more than an intern. She wanted access to the *WeWoreWhat* email account so she could manage things more easily. She wanted to become involved with the company's overarching strategy. She wanted to be my right hand.

Moe's requests caught me off guard. I have always believed in the old adage that if you want something done well, you should do it yourself. Delegating was not my strong suit. Most uberperfectionists struggle to relinquish control, and I was no different. I resisted her demands.

What I failed to see was that Moe is good at a lot of things I'm bad at—like managing a schedule. Her skill sets complement my own. I'm creative; she's organized. I'm moody; she's level headed. I'm yin; she's yang. We're opposites in almost every way except our work ethic (and our appreciation of a great tequila shot).

I was hesitant to integrate Moe into the business, and as a result, we had a hard time finding our flow. That might not have mattered back when things were slow, but it created *chaos* as soon as we got busy. Brand partnership opportunities were missed because we thought the other one had responded. Outstanding payments that were owed to us slipped through the cracks. Honestly, it's a wonder we got anything done.

The fact that we were such good friends only complicated things further. It's difficult enough to manage someone when you're as young as I was at the time. Keep in mind Moe is two years my junior, and I was in my early twenties. We were children trying to run a company and run New York City. When you're essentially growing up with your employee, and partying with her every night—it's almost impossible to find the balance between friend and boss. I won't lie to you: things between us got tense. Not quite like Jay-Z and Solange post–Boom Boom Room, but still bad.

There was no separation between our friendship and our work relationship. We would get into fights at clubs because one of us had too much to drink and forgot the next day's big photo shoot. We were kids making kid mistakes.

I had always known Moe planned to study abroad in Italy. When the time came, it seemed like a natural break—a chance for some space. We could decide if we wanted to keep working together when she got back. I had also always regretted my own inability to study abroad and wanted her to have that quintessential college experience. (Even though I travel the world all the time now, I had barely left the country at this point in my life.) I also worried that if we didn't take some space now, Moe and I might never be able to recover our relationship.

Since Moe was going to be gone for four months, I would need to find and train a replacement. I thought I needed a true intern—someone to do my bidding without challenging me. The anti-Moe. I was wrong.

Moe probably hadn't even deplaned in Florence before I realized my mistake. I didn't need just any old intern. I needed *her*. Someone who could build *WeWoreWhat* alongside me.

As I'm sure you have already realized, I have a very particular personality. People either get me, or they don't. Moe gets me. Her skills complement mine. I always knew that, but it took losing her to realize just how valuable that was.

When Moe got back from Florence at the end of the semester, I gave her a promotion, a raise, and, yes, access to the *WeWoreWhat* email. That was the day she stopped being an intern and started being my partner. Actually, in many ways, Moe has ended up more my boss than the other way around.

I've thought a lot about why I had such a hard time sharing responsibilities. I wonder if this, too, can be traced back to my childhood, which left me with this immense pressure to be independent. I've felt a wariness of relying on people, maybe because I didn't know if they'd be there the next day. While it's true my independence has served me well in many ways, it has also hindered me. When you find someone who is so completely on your wavelength, why not let them help you move your business forward?

I quickly learned the importance of finding a business partner whose strengths are the complete opposite of mine. And treating them well. The difference between being someone who happens to own a small business and being a true entrepreneur is realizing that you need good people in your corner. All of that is nothing, though, if you don't learn how to delegate.

My gut instinct has been to micromanage. I pride myself on doing everything myself. When I don't know how to do something, I figure it out. (It's why I'm taking start-up classes now, despite being a tech founder and CEO—I want to learn.)

Over the past eight years, my responsibilities as the leader of *WeWoreWhat* have become more complex. I now manage four full-time employees and countless contractors. I have been forced to accept that I don't have the time to do it all. If I want to be an effective leader, I will have to trust my team and learn to let go. As for Moe, we've built (the start of) an empire together and have pioneered an industry that quite frankly didn't exist before. Just like any relationship (because after all, she is my work wife), we will continue to grow and learn together. She's my not-so-secret weapon, and sharing the reins only makes me a stronger and more effective CEO.

Live With a Stranger…
and Then Move

It is a New York rite of passage to live with a complete stranger at least once. I met mine via mutual friends. We were introduced at a Nolita bar called Sweet & Vicious, about a month after I dropped out of FIT. Her name was Caitlin.

I hadn't been planning to move. But then Jess and Chelsea threw a major wrench into my plans when they decided to move to the Upper East Side, where the rent was cheaper and the apartments were bigger. There was no way in *hell* I was moving uptown. To this day, I maintain that the *only* reason to travel above Fourteenth Street is to eat at the Polo Bar, shop at Barney's (RIP), and visit the Met during its annual costume exhibit.

People couldn't understand why I was so sad to give up such a small apartment. (How I managed that many months with multiple roommates and a single bathroom, I'll never know.) Still, it was my first apartment in New York City—where I started *WeWoreWhat*. It had sentimental value.

More than that, I had *just* asked my dad to help me make rent while I focused on my blog. I had sworn up and down that there would be no unforeseen expenses. A move was definitely *not* included in my new budget. Not wanting to ask for any more money from my parents, I set about finding an apartment that didn't cost a penny more than where I was living at the moment.

I would have loved to live alone, but a studio apartment in Manhattan can cost up to four thousand per month—even in the most inconvenient locations. There was no question that I would need a roommate if I wanted to stay within my budget. It's a sad reality that most New Yorkers can't afford their own place until they're either dead or married. Another problem? Your lease will probably never be up at the same moment as someone you actually want to live with.

I began asking around, investigating whether anyone in my extended circle needed to move. I wrote numerous Facebook posts about how "clean" and "responsible" I was, like a twisted version of online dating. Eventually, a mutual friend introduced me to Caitlin as "the only girl as intense as me." (That my most dramatic friend was the one who recommended her probably should have been a red flag.)

At first, everything seemed great. Caitlin was a fiery Brazilian Jew who also wanted to live in the West Village and liked to go out every night. She had a gorgeous boyfriend who promised to set me up with his friends. After that trial night together at Sweet & Vicious, Caitlin and I decided we were ready to go apartment hunting together.

Looking for the perfect place to live in New York City is akin to hunting for diamond in a pile of horse shit. It's probably not there, but you need to dig through a ton of crap before you can know for sure. You will tour four-hundred-square-foot studios that feature bathtubs in the kitchen, one bedrooms where you can touch opposite walls at the same time, and "historic" lofts with high ceilings but plumbing that hasn't been updated since 1853. New Yorkers always have to choose between space and location, elevator and walk-up, natural light versus an updated kitchen. Only the incredibly wealthy can have it all.

And when you *do* manage to find an apartment that fits your criteria? You better have your checkbook in hand, because chances are there are already fifteen other people applying for it. You want five minutes to debate whether the Chinese restaurant on the ground floor with a C health rating might be a problem? Tough titties—the place is already gone, and now you have to live in Bushwick.

I thought my criteria were simple: I wanted an apartment that was south of Fourteenth Street, north of Canal Street, and west of Broadway. It had to be big enough to host an epic afterparty and cozy enough for a night at home watching *The Bachelor*. A doorman was also a must because my business was growing, in addition to safety concerns, I was receiving packages on a nearly constant basis. And don't even get me started on the need for more closet space.

Caitlin and I spent about a week looking at places with a Realtor. We toured one hundred duds before finding this *adorable* two bed two bath on Bleecker Street—an address that meant we'd be squarely nestled in the Greenwich Village neighborhood. The only reason it was even available and within our price range was because the previous rent-controlled tenant had died of old age.

Caitlin was comfortable with me paying a little more for the bigger room with the en suite bath. (I was fine sharing an apartment with a stranger, but *not*, under any circumstances, a bathroom.) We decided to fill out an application on the spot. Sure, we barely knew each other. But things seemed to be going our way.

The first thing I realized after moving in with Caitlin was that she ate Kraft Mac & Cheese for dinner every night. She paired each boxed meal with a forty-ounce bottle of beer and consumed the lot on the floor in front of our tiny television. Don't ask me *how* she maintained such a tight little body. I guess you can't beat those Brazilian genes.

The weird eating habits I could live with. But the next thing I noticed about Caitlin was a little bit more of a problem. Remember the hot boyfriend I mentioned earlier? The one I was hoping would introduce me to his friends? Well, he and Caitlin would get in screaming fights practically every night. I would lie awake listening to them argue over the most mundane things—what bar they should go to, if she'd been flirting with some guy, which one of them had forgotten to lock the front door. They yelled over each other more than Fox News commentators.

The problem was that Caitlin was an angry drunk. And as time passed, and she got more comfortable in our roommate relationship, she started to turn that anger on me. She would yell and throw tantrums like a toddler. I desperately wanted to move, but wouldn't have the money until *WeWoreWhat* started bringing in more.

And then one night, I came back from a bar called Wilfie & Nell with a few friends. Like a good roommate, I texted Caitlin on the way to let her know I was having people over. She replied and seemed fine with it at the time.

But about thirty minutes after we arrived, Caitlin came flying into the living room, screaming in Portuguese that no one understood. She finally switched to English and demanded that everyone "get the fuck out of her apartment." She was hysterical—almost frightening.

As my friends shuffled (a.k.a. sprinted) toward the door, I put my hands on Caitlin's shoulders in an effort to calm her down. The next thing I know, she broke my grip and started repetitively punching the wall, only inches away from my head. Panicked, I tried to follow my friends out of the apartment. She slammed the door full force on my hand, catching my fingers on the wood. To this day, it remains one of the most physically painful things I've experienced.

That was the day I decided I was done with roommates. Never again would I live with anyone I wasn't sleeping with. And until then, I was going to live *alone*.

Define Your Own Value

Iwill never forget the first time I attended New York Fashion Week. I was fourteen years old, and my dad had snagged two tickets to the Milly show. It took weeks to plan my outfit, scouring my teenage closet for anything that could possibly pass as one of the brand's designs. (In a dream world, I would have worn something Milly to the show, but my high school allowance permitted little more than a trip to the movie theater.)

This life-changing experience took place during a time that people call the glory days of New York Fashion Week, a.k.a. the 1990s and early 2000s. All of the shows still took place at Bryant Park. Instagram didn't exist. And all the future influencers were still at home reading *CosmoGirl*. Except for me, the lucky one who was going to experience the kind of old school show Anna Wintour still dreams about.

Of course, I didn't care that my dad and I were seated in the last row (behind every socialite, editor, and buyer). I was just happy to be there, in the presence of all those glamorous models and the gorgeous clothes. I propped my eyes open and tried not to blink, afraid of missing anything. The music got louder, the spotlights brightened, and the catwalk that changed my life began.

After the show, my dad took me to dinner at the Bryant Park Grill, an eatery that's long graced the back of the New York Public Library. I was too excited to stop talking. Bites of my Cobb salad flew everywhere as I pledged, "Someday, I am going to sit front row at a show just like *that*." I would wear head-to-toe designer duds and charm fashion's upper crust with the greatest of ease.

Fast-forward seven years, and I made that dream a reality.

You've already read about how I got my start snapping photos outside of the shows. As the event grew and more designers started to show, they moved Fashion Week to Lincoln Center. My first actual invitation, however, didn't come until 2013 when Mercedes-Benz made me their first official ambassador of New York Fashion Week. (Mercedes had been a longtime Fashion Week sponsor.) This meant I would attend all the shows as a representative of the car brand, documenting my experiences along the way. This guaranteed me a front row at every show and backstage access to interview the designers. After each day, I would film video content with Mercedes's team to discuss what trends I saw and which designers I loved. And what a moment this was.

In the seven years since my first *real* Fashion Week, the New York shows have gone through several iterations. The general concept has remained the same since 1943: to elevate American designers to the same status as those in London, Paris, and Milan—cities that already had their own Fashion Weeks. It wasn't until 1993, however, that the shows were consolidated to a single location in Bryant Park, and then later to Lincoln Center. This kept attendees from having to run all over the city, and meant designers didn't have to produce their shows from scratch. Brands could synergize their budgets for the tent, security, sound, etc.

Since then, the number of shows at New York Fashion Week has skyrocketed from fifty to nearly three hundred, making it impossible to host them all in a single venue. Designers are now expected to find their own locations. A lot of them gravitate toward places like Spring Studios, but I'm also just as likely to receive an invite to a carnival, an airport hangar, an old bank in the Financial District, or even an unmarked warehouse in Brooklyn. (I'm looking at you, Alexander Wang).

New York Fashion Week has been forced to redefine itself constantly, which has either ruined it or kept it chic, depending on who you ask.

Then came the age of the influencer, which changed Fashion Week forever. Shows used to have their own hierarchy. Editors, socialites, and movie stars sat in front, with buyers beside them and everyone else in the rows behind that. These days, much of the front row is dominated by a bunch of newer Instagram stars focused on giving their followers an inside look at the shows in real time (much to the chagrin of the old guard).

As can be expected, the disruption of the long-standing social order has created a lot of tension in the fashion industry. Some traditional magazine editors have complained about the number of influencers being invited. We've also been accused of lingering outside to take street style photos in what has not-so-lovingly been referred to as the Street Style Circus. (It's a clusterfuck of photographers and Instagram girls who pretend they don't notice the photographers.)

I've participated in the Street Style Circus more times than I care to admit. The photos might look candid when you see them in magazines or online, but in reality we'll cross the street three or four times just to make sure the photographer got the shot. Dozens of girls might be strutting at any given time, all jockeying for prime positions on *ELLE* and Vogue.com street style roundups. (I have since stopped caring and head to my car as quickly as possible.)

The sheer number of "cool girl" influencers these days have made scoring a seat at Fashion Week ultracompetitive. The standard used to be that you received an invitation if you worked with the brand or were friends with the publicists. All anyone cared about was your style, your relationships, and your following.

For those of us who do manage to be seated—and in the coveted front row—now we have to worry about our seat's position. (I get a headache just thinking about this.) I'll never forget the first time I was ditched for a "better" companion.

I had been close friends with this British blogger for years (let's call her Anna), and we'd decided to grab coffee before attending the Tibi show together. We had just arrived and found our seats when Anna spotted an up-and-coming French influencer a few seats over. She did a quick Google search and discovered the girl had just been featured in French *Vogue*, a.k.a. the holy grail of fashion. She disappeared "to go to the bathroom," and the next thing I knew there was a buyer from Neiman's sitting next to me—which was cool, but not the seatmate who had been assigned to me. Anna, of course, was now sitting beside said French girl in hopes that they would be photographed together. She avoided my gaze and pretended like nothing had happened.

This might sound like a small offense, but I had already spent a full week of fashion shows with stuff like this happening. I like to see the best in people, but Fashion Week brings out a side to my peers that I don't always like. It's draining. So once the Tibi show was over, I avoided the Street Style Circus and ran straight to my car—able to hold back my tears until the door was shut behind me. This wasn't what I had signed up for.

Sure, our industry is ultimately about visual appeal, but that afternoon felt like a bad replay of high school. I didn't want to believe fashion really was *The Devil Wears Prada*, but I was quickly learning that some aspects of that movie were unfortunately true.

There is one other thing about Fashion Week that's worth noting: it has to do with pulling looks to wear to the designer's shows. It's so exciting when a brand wants to dress you. Who doesn't want a chance to wear next season's looks before they hit the stores? But, unfortunately, the clothes we can pull are usually only sample sizes (0, 2). I, of course, am not a sample size. My body simply isn't built that way. Unable to fit into pants or skirts, I'm often left with loose-fitting dresses or tops. (Which has actually worked to my advantage, as my followers love to see how I style the designer pieces with my own.) It's no one's fault, but that doesn't make it any less difficult. It has made me feel insecure. No woman wants to be too big for anything.

There are still so many things I love about New York Fashion Week. It's this special moment when I get to reunite with true friends from around the globe—girls whom I wouldn't get to see if not at this event twice a year. (You know you're real friends when you talk about everything *but* fashion.) There are also these special runway shows where the fashion is so good it sends chills down my spine. So good that it reminds me why I fucking love my job, why I love fashion.

It's great to support brands that are reimagining Fashion Week. Take Rebecca Minkoff, who famously unveiled a "see now, buy now" show where everything that came down the runway was available in stores right after the show. Rebecca's initiative was so successful, and so much more in tune with the way people actually shop, that other designers have followed suit.

I don't know what New York Fashion Week will look like in the future. What I do know is that I constantly question its value and need. The jury is still out for me.

Is Fashion Week still about fashion? Should I spend my entire year angling to get invited to the hottest shows? No. Will I cry if I get a bad seat assignment? Not anymore. Will I spend fifteen minutes outside taking photos with street style photographers? Absolutely not.

I have so much more to give than just being a street style star or a front row regular. I have a new way of doing business. I have reach and a deep connection with my followers. I have selling power and the conversion rates to prove it. I know my value, and no one else gets to determine it except me. Especially not the brands deciding whether or not to invite me to their shows.

I'm going to focus on what I always loved about Fashion Week, that it's fun, social, and inspiring—I've learned to value what matters most. It's how I show up, how I choose to behave. I've learned to really appreciate and give my all to the shows that I am invited to. And when the show ends, I will walk straight back to my car with my head held high. Because no one—not a publicist, not a magazine, not a fellow influencer—gets to determine my value except me.

Use Your Time Wisely

Paris Fashion Week is everything that New York Fashion Week is not. Whereas New York Fashion Week is constantly reimagining the event, the French Fashion Federation hasn't changed a thing since its first shows in 1973. You can tell Paris Fashion Week is the most important, because they always get to go last—after New York, London, and Milan, in that order. It is the single most important event in our industry—like Easter, Hanukkah, and New Year's combined.

French designers do everything by the book, which, of course, means it's almost impossible to get an invite. Even someone like me, who has more than two million followers, struggles to get attention from French brands. In all my years as an influencer, I have never been invited to a single show for Chanel, Chloé, or Dior. The number of emails I have received explaining that they "can't accommodate me this season" or are "at full capacity" are laughable.

French brands don't care about your following; they care about tradition. They want to fill their front rows with European girls whose pedigrees put the Queen of England to shame. (Side note: Elizabeth actually has attended London Fashion Week). In order to be invited to the Louis Vuitton show, you better be a Parisian social-ite with two dozen recent appearances in French *Vogue*. (Print, not online.) And if you've worked with a ton of commercial brands, oof, forget it. A heathen Long Islander like me doesn't stand a chance.

I guess I understand where these brands are coming from. They're seen as uber-aspirational and try to maintain a mystique. But I'd be lying if I didn't say part of me still struggles to understand why they wouldn't want me—someone with so much quantifiable selling power and reach. Someone who is a true fan of the brands and has supported them by purchasing pieces over the years. An American girl who reaches a primarily American audience (of shoppers, duh).

I attended Paris Fashion Week for the first time in 2014, al-though I use the word "attended" loosely because I wasn't invited to a single show. Instead, I stuffed myself into a tiny hotel room with two other girls and spent the week living off baguettes from the local patisserie. So why was I there? To attend re-sees and events, where I could get face time with brands and PRs and start those relationships. My goal, other than to create content, was to ingratiate myself with the French.

A few years of fearless networking later, and as my blog continued to grow, I was invited to sit front row at Balmain. That same season, I was also blessed by the gods at Louis Vuitton and Lanvin. Chanel still wouldn't toss a tweed in my direction, but that trip was still one of the moments that put me on the global map. (On the flip side, it's one of my greatest regrets to have not seen a Chanel show while Karl Lagerfeld was alive.)

I had spent years of my life campaigning to get into these shows. So you can imagine my surprise when I posted the content to my Instagram, exclamation points everywhere, only to find that my followers didn't seem to really care. Turns out they care more about seeing what I had worn to the shows instead, who I had seen, and how I would style the runway pieces when they came out. If they wanted stock photos of whatever came down the runway, they could turn to *Vogue Runway*. The discovery that my followers gravitated more to me and my behind-the-scenes content than to couture was humbling.

Paris Fashion Week is still one of the most important events for forging relationships in the international fashion industry. If you're a rising blogger, I do recommend going. Fortunately I have flown myself across the ocean for more than six calendar years—which means twelve Fashion Weeks—and can finally give myself a little break. Now, I try to only attend if I have a paying job with a brand like FWRD (Revolve's big sister and designer site).

I've had to train myself to think in terms of an ROI (return on investment), to make sure I was getting the bang for my buck.

Obviously, I would be on the next plane to Charles de Gaulle if Chanel suddenly decided to invite me. (If any of their publicists are reading this, I will literally trade both of my dogs for a seat. Maybe. Probably.)

But at the end of the day, time is money. It's an entrepreneur's most precious commodity, the only thing they can't make more of. Over the years, I've had to learn how to prioritize my time. Whether Fashion Week is or isn't worth the time commitment… well, that depends on what I have going on at that moment.

Intro Continued...
the Elevator Hunk

You heard about it in my intro, but this is the story of how I started writing this very book.

Most New Yorkers have a love/hate relationship with our neighbors. On the one hand, they are the people who live closest to us—the ones who would (hopefully) share their water during a natural disaster and alert the police to any strange smells coming from our apartment. And yet an urgent email that prevents us from chatting always seems to come in whenever we run into them in the mail room. Such is life in Manhattan.

There is, however, one reason to talk to your neighbor: when they're a really hot guy. Dating someone in your building is like having Postmates for penis. You don't even need to put on shoes in order to satisfy your cravings.

After all the drama (Michael, dropping out of school) that came with 2013, I pledged that 2014 would be the Year of Danielle. Time to focus on myself and my brand. And in order to make sure I didn't get distracted, I decided romantic relationships were off limits. Casual dating was fine, but absolutely nothing serious. The second I thought about bringing someone home to meet Grandma Joyce, they had to go.

At first, it was hard to retrain my brain. I've always been a relationship girl (in case you haven't noticed). But I had just traded my studio for a one bedroom loft and could distract myself by decorating my new rental apartment. And *We Wore What* kept me very busy.

It took me until mid-May to ignore the voice in my head that screams "mate for life" and really embrace this new way of dating. But by summer, I had successfully learned how to deflect the commitment impulse. I was Teflon. I was still dating lots of guys and met all sorts of different people, but almost no one made it past the first date. It was freeing to let myself enjoy the company of men without the pressure that comes with a potential relationship. I could be completely myself without worrying about whether they'd call me the next day, because I sure wasn't.

I like to call this time period my "Samantha Summer."

My new apartment building, the Archive, was one of those quintessential New York landmarks that everyone seems to know. The building has historic significance, being the former home of the US Appraiser's Warehouse. The Archive is better known, however, as the home to Monica Lewinsky during the fallout from her notorious affair with President Bill Clinton. (Which, considering I was trying to be more sexually free, felt like a pretty good omen.)

I was a few weeks into my Samantha Summer when I noticed a REALLY HOT GUY had also moved into the building. (I'm using caps because that's just how good-looking he was.) He was a bit older than me—maybe midthirties—and had the kind of body that wouldn't look out of place in an underwear ad. It only took a few shared rides in the elevator before I was smitten. I was so obsessed, and talked about this guy so often, that my friends started to call him Elevator Hunk. (Although, to be fair, there was also Coffeeshop Cutie and Dry Cleaner Dude at the time.)

I like to make the first move on men, but there was something different about Elevator Hunk. We always happened to run into each other at the worst times—during my walks of shame or after a particularly sweaty Soul Cycle class. (There's nothing worse than that postspin beet-red face.) Why could he never run into me when I was on my way to a photo shoot? What about the thousands of times each week that I waited outside my building for a black car to take me to an event?

Elevator Hunk probably thought I was a not-so-hot mess. After he saw me trip up the stairs after a few too many tequilas, I wrote him off as one of the ones who got away. Still, I started carrying an extralarge pair of Chloé sunglasses with me everywhere I went... *just in case* we bumped into each other around the neighborhood.

One day, I saw Elevator Hunk with a dog that I'd never seen before. I eavesdropped on his phone conversation just long enough to hear my crush explain this was Bonnie, his new rescue pup. Apparently, Bonnie was having a hard time adjusting to her new home. As luck would have it, I had also somewhat recently gotten a dog—an adorable French bulldog named Bleecker. He was an impulse purchase after Michael and I broke up. What better way to be consoled than by a puppy?

It was time for baby Bleecker to learn how to wingman.

Over the next few days, I took Bleecker on an exorbitant number of walks in hopes that we would run into Elevator Hunk. I was also sure to always look banging in case my dreams came true. (My favorite Alo Yoga leggings—the ones that kinda suck me in—got a lot of wear that week.)

Eventually, we did run into Elevator Hunk and Bonnie. It happened in (where else?) the elevator just as Bleecker and I were returning from a sunset stroll along the Hudson River. Thank *God* I had attended a press dinner at Cafe Cluny and was looking extra fly in my Acne blazer and Frame skinny jeans.

The dogs started jumping all over, trying to investigate each other's nether regions. I found my mind wondering what it would be like to do the same thing to the gorgeous man standing next to me…

When Elevator Hunk spoke, I was jolted out of my fantasy. His voice was lightly accented and as seductive, even though he was only asking the standard dog questions: "Boy or girl? What's his name? How old?"

As we ticked closer to the fourth floor, where I obviously already knew Elevator Hunk lived from my stalking, I began to panic that I was going to lose my chance. I had been handed a silver plate opportunity to make the first move. Don't blow it, Danielle! As the doors closed, I managed to force out the words, "We should have a puppy playdate sometime."

"Sure," he said with a lopsided grin before disappearing down the hall with Bonnie in tow.

I was thrilled but couldn't shake the feeling that I had forgotten something. Just as I reached my floor, I realized: we hadn't exchanged phone numbers. Fuck. It had taken me this long to run into him under the right circumstances, and I'd totally blown it.

I'll be honest: I'm not proud of what I did next. I rode the elevator straight back to the lobby and begged my doorman to spill Elevator Hunk's apartment number. (In hindsight, it's probably highly illegal that he told me.) Then I sprinted back to my apartment armed with new information, scrawled my digits on a piece of paper, and slid the note under his door. He was either going to find this incredibly hot or incredibly creepy.

I ran back upstairs and turned on the HBO series *True Blood* as distraction. If anything could take my mind off the past hour, it would be a half-naked Alexander Skarsgård. I willed myself not to stare at my phone, remembering my mom's words that a "watched pot never boils." (Except it totally does, but whatever. It's a saying.)

Elevator Hunk texted about an hour later.

Elevator Hunk, 8:56 p.m.: Nice to meet you neighbor. Let's go for that walk soon.

Conveniently, I was leaving for Los Angeles the next morning and thus had an A+ response.

Me, 9:08 p.m.: I'm leaving tomorrow for a week. Was about to take Bleecker out before I hit the hay. Want to go on a night walk?

Elevator Hunk, 9:08 p.m.: Lobby in five?

Hell. Freaking. Yeah.

I tousled my hair, slapped on some concealer (Mac Fluid Fix in NC20) and slipped on a tank top so tight, I'm pretty sure I bought it before going through puberty. Then I had a pep talk with Bleecker. "You better be ready to work it, little guy," I told him. "Samantha is in the building."

Elevator Hunk and I met in the lobby, then ambled up Greenwich Avenue en route to the neighborhood dog park at the start of the Bleecker Street shopping district. He told me about his job (model), his age (thirty-two), and his family (back home in Italy). The news that he was both foreign *and* actually successful only made me swoon that much harder.

It had started to drizzle by the time we reached the park. No one, however, seemed to care—especially not the pups, who chased each other with reckless abandon. As for me…the rain only added to the evening's romantic atmosphere.

As the weather worsened, Elevator Hunk unbuttoned his plaid shirt to hold over our heads as a makeshift umbrella. (Unfortunately, he had a tee on underneath.) But as the rain pounded and his white undershirt got wet, I could start to make out the definition of his perfect pecs. The guy was a model, for crying out loud. No, I wasn't going to marry him. But I *could* see what he looked like without any clothes on.

We stayed at the park until it really started to pour. On our walk back to the Archive, I noticed that Elevator Hunk seized any opportunity to make physical contact—touching my arm and knocking his hip against mine. Somehow this transient physical contact was so much sexier than if he laid one on me.

But then we paused under some scaffolding, which always seems to be present in Manhattan. Elevator Hunk turned and asked, "What else can we do in the rain?" Jokingly, I answered, "Dance!" He asked again. I replied, "Sing." He asked *again*. This time, I knew the answer he wanted. "Make out?" He must have liked that option, because the next thing I knew I was pushed up against a brick wall with his hands in my hair and his tongue down my throat.

Eventually, we made it home—giggly, aroused, and soaking wet. The rain had stopped, but our clothes had yet to dry, and the flirtatious atmosphere lingered. Elevator Hunk actually missed his floor twice because we couldn't stop pawing at each other in the elevator.

As Bleecker and I dried off in my apartment a few minutes later, my phone buzzed with a text.

Elevator Hunk, 11:16 p.m.: That was fun. Hope you're not too wet.

Truth be told, I was. I consulted my inner Samantha and told him to come over. Fuck my early flight. This was worth it.

You know what happened next—as soon as he left my bed the next morning I grabbed my phone to text my friends. Wrote the experience down as a story. Wrote about my entire Samantha Summer as a series of stories. Decided to write a book. Then didn't.

Even still, I have to credit Elevator Hunk with jump-starting this entire project. It may have taken me years to actually publish the thing, but without that evening's spontaneity, this book would never have existed.

Kiss a Lot of Frogs...

I should probably admit that not every moment of my Samantha Summer was earth-shattering sex with Italian male models. Most of the men I dated during those months were downright duds. But, as my mom always told me, you have to kiss a lot of frogs before you find your Prince Charming. And the best thing about casual dating? Not only do you learn so much about yourself (and what you want in a partner), but you also get to be fun and spontaneous.

To recall the worst first date of my life, I will have to back up to the start of that summer. Around Memorial Day weekend of 2013. Some friends had rented a house in Bridgehampton to both distract me from stewing over Michael *and* celebrate my twenty-first birthday. Still reeling from my breakup but ready to dip my toe into the casual dating pool, I decided that flirting with cute guys at the Southampton Social Club sounded like just the ticket.

As with any weekend in the Hamptons for someone unable to splurge for a Blade chopper, our trip started with a long drive on the Long Island Expressway. Chelsea was in the driver's seat, having borrowed her mom's minivan for the occasion. As we cruised up the Sunset Highway, I painted my nails and wondered if we'd ever make it our destination. (The roads between New York and the Hamptons are always bottlenecked with angry real estate brokers worried about their reservation at Nick and Toni's. It's extremely unpleasant.)

But for whatever reason, traffic was minimal that day. (Probably because we'd left at 10:00 a.m., before even those with summer Fridays got off work.) We merged onto Sunset Highway, and there was only one other vehicle on the road: a vintage black convertible. I'd love to tell you what kind of car it was, but I was too focused on the man driving the car to notice much else. (Also, full disclosure, I'm shit when it comes to cars. I'm a fashion girl, not a motorhead.)

I begged Chelsea to drive faster to give me a better look. As we edged our way closer, I realized that there were actually…*three* hot guys inside the car, each wearing a black T-shirt and black sunglasses. Their entire appearance was perfectly monochrome. *Who were these men? And why didn't we know them?*

Per usual, I decided to make the first move using…a note. (Holla, Michael! Holla, Elevator Hunk!) I scoured Chelsea's car for a piece of paper, eventually settling on the only thing I could find:

a vet bill for her Cavalier King Charles, Binky. Which, fine, would do in a pinch.

I ripped off the bottom and scrawled my name and number on Binky's bill, then told Chelsea to floor it. (Fortunately, Chelsea was the kind of friend willing to die in order for me to meet men.) As our van struggled to speed up, the guys noticed what was happening and rolled down their windows. I leaned out of the minivan, my upper body dangerously exposed, and handed off the note just as our car reached the Bridgehampton exit.

Success.

The first text came in a few hours later. It was from the car's driver, Sam. (Although the honest truth is that I've forgotten the guy's name and am using Sam as a placeholder.) Sam wanted to take me out for dinner when we were back in the city. I accepted the invitation, basking in the glow of such an outrageous victory. Picking up a guy on the highway? Who does that? It was the perfect, scandalous way to start my Samantha Summer.

The next Tuesday, I strolled out of my apartment building at 8:45 p.m.—exactly fifteen minutes after Sam had told me to be ready and waiting. (As my grandma Joyce says, "A lady is never exactly on time.") I scanned Greenwich Avenue for Sam's convertible, but it was nowhere to be seen. There was, however, a hulking Harley motorcycle. And who should be leaning against it except Sam?

"Um, what's that?" I asked tentatively, gesturing to the black bike.

"Your chariot, and it awaits," he replied. (I should have cancelled the date just for him being that cheesy.)

"You're crazy if you think I'm getting on that thing. Even if we don't die in a crash, my mom will kill me for riding a motorcycle."

There was no way in hell I was getting on that bike. No. Way. In. Hell.

But Sam's smile was pretty cute. His jeans also had the perfect amount of visible wear—the knee fades that denim brands spend crazy money trying to mimic. Oh yeah, and he had a beard. Plus, the Samantha Summer was supposed to be about meeting people and trying new things. It was time to turn off my inner monologue and roll with the punches.

The next few minutes were like an out of body experience. I had told Sam I would get on the bike, but only if we didn't go far. So you can imagine my surprise when, just ten minutes later, we were barreling across the Williamsburg Bridge at what felt like break-neck speeds.

I was beyond fucking scared. My fingernails dug into Sam's side, which he interpreted as excitement—encouragement to drive faster. I, however, was just holding on for dear life. At one point, I glanced over the bridge railing, saw the ominous depths of the East River, and imagined my body plummeting toward the water.

Even as my life flashed before my eyes, I began to feel oddly... exhilarated. Normally, I dated the kind of guys who would pick me up in black cars (or at least a yellow cab). But here I was on the back of a motorcycle, enjoying the twinkling lights and the warm summer air. It was so unlike my usual dates that it felt like a dream.

And you can't die in dreams, right? I was on a bike, on a bridge, with a stranger.

"Fuck it," I thought and flung my arms out wide in an homage to *Titanic.* "I'm flying!"

Turns out Sam was a chef. He took me to the Brooklyn restaurant where he worked and placed me at the chef's counter, sending an endless number of small plates in my direction. Only after I announced that I couldn't take another bite did he agree to stop feeding me and head to a dive bar around the corner, where we enjoyed a few drinks and a pretty public make out. Around 1:00 a.m., I told Sam it was time to drive me home. I had a shoot the next day, and it was already way past my bedtime.

By the time we rode back, I already considered myself an expert motorcycle companion. I strapped on the helmet and hopped on without prompting. I let myself relax and felt the tequila pulsing through my veins. I enjoyed it all—the air on my face, the stunning Manhattan skyline. The heavy petting we'd engaged in only a few moments prior paled in comparison to this kind of adrenaline.

Of course, that's when it all went to shit.

Sam exited the Williamsburg Bridge and pulled onto the FDR highway, which frames the east border of Manhattan. The road goes down and around the island's butt (a.k.a. the Financial District) before turning into the West Side Highway. But unlike the Westside Highway, the FDR is raised, which means there's nowhere to go between exits. Not even a shoulder or sidewalk on which to pull over.

So it was particularly terrifying when the motorcycle sputtered to a stop midway between exits. "What the hell is going on?" I asked Sam, a note of fear in my voice.

"I think we're out of gas," Sam replied, explaining that he'd been so caught up in the evening, he'd forgotten to fill up in Brooklyn. "Oh, and my phone is dead."

Cool, cool, cool. Tight, tight, tight.

I scanned the highway for any signs of life, or refuge, but found only a lamppost. I leapt off the bike and sprinted toward that post like my life depended on it—probably the fastest I've ever run in my life. (Thank God it was two o'clock in the morning and there were barely any cars.) I wrapped myself around the lamppost like a monkey and told Sam I wouldn't let go until a vehicle arrived to take me home. He could stand in the middle of the highway like an idiot if he wanted, but I was staying right here.

"I don't want to leave you, but one of us needs to find gas," Sam explained. "So either I can go or you can."

"Um, I'm just going to stay here with my new best friend lamppost," I said. "You come back with reinforcements, and I'll watch your bike."

So Sam left his motorcycle stranded in the middle of the highway and his date stranded on a lamppost.

In my defense, I tried to wait for him. But when Sam hadn't returned twenty minutes later, I decided it was time to call an Uber. I shimmied my phone out of my butt pocket and opened the app.

The understandably confused driver called two seconds later. "I'm sorry, but where are you? Your pin makes it seem like you're in the middle of the highway."

"I'm on the FDR between exits one and two," I shouted in a panic. "Like literally *on* the highway. You'll recognize me because I'm the girl clinging to a lamppost like an asshole."

Thankfully, the driver arrived a few minutes later. (Actually the only time Uber's ETA has ever been accurate.) I hopped in the Toyota Camry with a sense of relief and watched Sam's motorcycle fade in the rearview mirror (I had walked it over as close to the edge as possibly before ditching). He never contacted me, and I never contacted him.

This isn't the story of how I met my future husband. It is, however, one of my favorite cocktail party anecdotes—the tale I tell when asked about dating in Manhattan. Sometimes the best dates become the worst, and thus give you the best stories. So say yes to new experiences and…make sure your phone is charged before getting on motorcycles with strangers at 2:00 a.m.

And Then Meet a Nice Guy

Only at the *very* end of my Samantha Summer did I let my friends start setting me up on blind dates. I wasn't looking for a relationship and didn't want to have a casual fling with anyone in my circle—someone I might have to make polite small talk with at a baby shower three years down the line. These were meant to be months of freedom—a period of self-discovery. Hence any potential suitor needed to have at least two degrees of separation.

After a summer of dating randos, though, I was finally ready for my first setup. The target was a Waspy investment banker named Rick, who happened to be the cousin of a good friend. We had met a few times at parties and always gotten along, despite the fact that Rick was one of those Manhattan men with too much money and no real work ethic. He was both well-mannered and well-groomed—his nails often had a more recent manicure than my own—but unlikely to become the love of my life.

Then Rick invited me to spend Labor Day on his parents' two-hundred-foot yacht…and, well, I couldn't help but swipe right on the situation.

It wasn't hard to convince my pals Tara and Hannah to tag along for the weekend. Seventy-two hours of boats, boys, and booze—all for free. What's not to love? (Except for the sun damage, but that's why God invented spray tans.)

I called Tara and Hannah because they were my best wing women. Tara is our smartest, most responsible friend, but also very fun. Hannah, on the other hand, is the quintessential blond bombshell. She's as naturally beautiful and free spirited as Serena Van Der Woodsen. Maybe more. Together, the three of us would be unstoppable.

We picked up a supply of Montauk Beer Summer Ale and did some very on-the-nose pregame drinking on the eastbound train. We arrived at the Montauk Yacht Club three hours later tipsy and ready to party. I shook back my newly cropped blond hair (which seemed like a great idea at the time, but never again will I chop above the shoulder) and strode up the plank, confident in my spray tan and Reformation minidress.

Rick appeared in a panic. "Oh no. Oh no. Could you please take off your shoes? My parents just refinished the teak deck."

And with that single sentence, I knew Rick wasn't my guy. Yech. Still, he was impeccably courteous and offered us a drink before commencing his tour of the vessel. We sipped Wolffer Estate's "Summer in a Bottle" rosé as we wandered the boat's *five* bedrooms, one of which had been allocated to us.

Rick was happy to share more about himself. He came from one of those East Coast families who had gotten insanely rich off some insanely random invention. (I can't remember what, but let's say metal straws.)

My jaw kept dropping as Rick shuttled us from room to room. Here's how one international directory of superyachts describes his family's boat: "Her interior is in rich teak panelling, with a light and relaxed ambiance throughout. The main saloon features loose furniture in an informal setting with a cream coloured headliner and décor in tones of light blue."

You get the point.

As we emerged on the deck an hour later, my eyes blinking against the setting sun, I found myself unable to focus on the words now coming out of Rick's mouth…because I had just spotted a *ridiculously hot guy* relaxing in the hot tub. (Yes, the boat had a freaking open-air hot tub.)

Rick introduced him as Alex, one of his best friends from college. Alex was tall, like six-feet-five, dark, and handsome. He even had a thick beard. The only thing preventing him from being my dream guy was the lack of leather jacket, but I excused him considering he was in the water. It was as if he had been created in a factory just for me.

The feeling I experienced when I met Alex can only be described as whatever Jack felt when he first spotted Rose aboard the *Titanic*. I blushed, I giggled, I daydreamed about kissing his neck. Suffice it to say, I had a crush.

But Alex wasn't just handsome. He was also smart and considerate—the exact guy who could convince me to break my "no feelings" streak. I had met so many men during my Samantha Summer, but none with Alex's manners or charm. Just as an example, Alex made sure everyone at the dinner table had everything they needed before he sat down. Hell, he *cleared* the table along with the yacht's dozen or so employees. What twentysomething guy passes up a round of beer pong to *clean*?

There was just one little issue. I was there to be set up with Rick, who was kindly hosting my friends and me for the weekend. Assuming a flirtation with one of Rick's best friends was probably a faux pas, I did my best to ignore my feelings…and therefore ignore Alex himself. I acted as if he wasn't even on my radar (while of course stalking him out of the corner of my eye).

That night, I drank rosé and danced my ass off to Kygo's latest hit—because what else does one do in the Hamptons? When it was time for bed, I dodged Rick's advances and slept in the room with Tara and Hannah. (Sometimes a faked migraine *truly* is a girl's best friend.) I fell asleep thinking about Alex, whom I had barely spoken to all day.

I awoke the next morning feeling awkward and wondering how could I avoid Rick until Monday? I went into the kitchen for breakfast, ready to drown myself in humiliation hash browns. (Yes, I was so upset that I ate starches the same day I had to be in a bikini. Now, thankfully, I have infrared saunas and lymphatic drainage massages as provision.) But then halfway through my solo meal, who should walk in except Alex? My heart be still.

"Hey! We didn't really get a chance to meet yet. I'm Alex," he said with an extended hand. I found myself studying his fingers, which were big enough to get me thinking about the rest of his body.

"I know." I replied as we shook. "I think you beat me at beer pong last night? I'm Danielle."

"Rick told me you had a headache, so I found some Tylenol," he explained while revealing the two pills in his hand. At that moment, I could have been on a row-boat anywhere. It didn't matter where I was, the thought of someone being so thoughtful and kind was so much more than any yacht could offer.

By the time Alex and I finished our first cup of coffee, I had already named our first child and was wondering what our white picket fence would look like. (I'm not a suburb girl, but I could be for *this* guy.) My daydream ended abruptly, however, when a girl I didn't know sauntered in looking like she'd gotten some the night before. She placed her hands on Alex's shoulders and leaned in to kiss his cheek. The message was clear: Alex was spoken for. At least for this weekend.

But Alex must have felt something, too, because I found him making excuses to spend time alone with me. If I wanted a snack, he offered to walk me to the kitchen. If I asked to jet ski, he tagged along. I'll never forget the energy that pulsed between our touching bare legs as we sped across the Atlantic Ocean.

I wanted him so badly my body actually ached—a sensation only intensified by the fact that we could not be together that weekend. We could, however, be friends. Alex and I grew so close over the next thirty-six hours, in fact, that we jokingly called each other "hubby" and "wifey."

Then Monday morning rolled around, and it was time for Alex to take the jitney to JFK. Because, oh yeah. Alex lived in Chicago. The Midwest. The part of the country I had vacated one year prior. Joke of my fucking life. We exchanged numbers and a lingering hug goodbye, our feelings unspoken and unconsummated.

Over the next few days, Alex and I started to talk on the phone. Before I knew it, we were FaceTiming every night before bed. He seemed like someone with not only a good heart in his chest, but also a good head on his shoulders. He asked lots of questions about my career and was happy to talk about his own job in real estate investments. Every guy claims to be on the hunt for a serious girlfriend, but I actually believed Alex when he said it two weeks later.

It was kind of funny. Here I was, starting something with a guy I hadn't even kissed after a summer of casual flings. Physical chemistry had always been so important to me. But the fact that this courtship was chaste seemed like a good omen. We would become friends first and lovers second—something I had never tried before.

In late September, Alex made an excuse to come back to New York. He insisted he was "visiting his friends," but it had only been a few weeks since Labor Day weekend. We both knew I was the real reason for his visit. I spent ages preparing for his arrival. I cleaned my apartment, I got a Brazilian wax, I stopped binging on late night chocolate. (Oh, and I also got a colonic. Don't judge.)

Alex's visit happened to coincide with Rosh Hashanah, the Jewish New Year. I invited him to celebrate with my family, which I guess was a pretty bold move. But for some reason, it felt extremely normal.

My family always spends the holiday at Grandma Joyce's house, where she makes a massive meal of old-world favorites like latkes and matzo ball soup. Grandma Joyce, the matriarch of my mom's clan, may be eighty-seven but still acts like she's forty. She does her hair and makeup every day. More important, though, she's the one who decides the worthiness of any newcomer to the family. She's the person I respect most. If Alex was to be welcomed into the fold, he would have to pass Grandma Joyce's inspection.

Keep in mind that Alex and I still hadn't kissed, which some-how only made me more nervous to introduce him to my family. It was like I knew that he was going to be someone important in my life.

Obviously, my family loved Alex for all the same reasons that at-tracted me to him on Rick's yacht. When he met Grandma Joyce at her front door, he immediately reached out and shook her hand— no nerves in sight—and then helped her up the steps. When Alex asked if we needed help cooking, everyone in the kitchen visibly swooned. If anything, my family thought he might be too good for me. Not the other way around.

But Alex didn't make a move that entire day in Great Neck, not even when we took a gorgeous sunset walk along the Long Island Sound together. He wouldn't kiss me. Hell, he wouldn't even hold my hand. I started to wonder if I'd created our entire romance in my head. Were Alex and I really just friends? Was he about to ask me to help him find a girlfriend? For the first time in my life, I was afraid to make the first move.

Maybe Alex simply didn't like me *that* way. I had to admit that looks aside, Alex wasn't the kind of guy I normally dated. He was Midwestern, which to most New Yorkers means he was basically from another planet. He didn't know who Alan Cumming was, but could name every player on the Bulls season roster. And yet his grounded, easygoing nature was the perfect antidote to my high pressure lifestyle. He had an earnest smile and a tendency to call women "ma'am," regardless of their age. If Michael prided himself on knowing all the best after-hour clubs, Alex was just happy to know where the best cup of joe was. And maybe that was just what I needed.

Alex made me feel safe. I was simultaneously thrilled by him and confident in the idea that he would never hurt me. I wasn't about to give that up without a fight.

I decided to confront the situation in the car back to the city. "It's fine if you don't like me like that; I just need to know," I lied, ready to throw myself out of the Uber if he didn't reciprocate my feelings.

Alex looked at my frown and started laughing. "You're crazy impatient, you know. Can't we get to know each other before jumping into things?"

"Sure," I replied. "But I thought you should know that I don't want to be your friend."

Alex held my gaze, as if contemplating his next move. That's when our car pulled into the Midtown Tunnel and everything went dark. I couldn't see, but I could feel, Alex's lips meet mine. I'll never understand why he chose the back seat of a bumpy car to make his move—seriously, the Honda had no shocks—but the moment was perfect. Even our driver seemed thrilled at the prospect of new love blossoming in the back of his Civic.

Thus began our three-year relationship, with me finally—finally—finding a nice guy. It took one parental divorce, dozens of meaningless flings, and several failed relationships before I decided

I was worthy of someone that nice, but when I finally did…well, there was no going back. If I was going to be the most successful fashion blogger in the world, then I didn't have time to waste on assholes. I needed someone who would support me and help me grow, treat me like his queen. And that, at least for the time being, was Alex.

Admit When You're Wrong

Alex and I dated long distance for the first six months of our relationship. We tried to visit each other every two weeks, alternating between his city and mine. You would imagine separation would stall our fledgling romance, but it only made things that much more delicious when we could actually be together. We fell in love.

Funnily enough, I actually preferred visiting Alex in Chicago (even though my blog was on a rocket ship, and it was harder than ever to get away). Being in *his* city just seemed so sexy. Alex had never lived outside the Midwest, so he had more friends in the area than Leonardo DiCaprio has model ex-girlfriends. He was in constant demand, dodging invitations to parties so that we could dine at the best restaurants in the city's hot Fulton Market neighborhood. (I suggest Monteverde, Au Cheval, and Girl and the Goat.)

If Alex was the unofficial king of Chicago, then I was happy to be his foreign queen.

We had a great, if inconvenient, thing going. So you can imagine my surprise when, just six months into our young relationship, Alex suggested that he move to New York City. My gut reaction: If it ain't broke, don't fix it.

We talked about what a move would do to our relationship. I voiced my concerns about moving too fast, but Alex said all the right things. He insisted that he wasn't moving for me—not *just* for me, I should say. He had always planned on moving to New York at some point. His company even had an office he could transfer to in Manhattan. Meeting me had only speeded up a pre-existing timeline.

Of course, I wanted to see Alex more often. But I also worried about the pressure this move would put on our new love. Wasn't it too early for us to make such major life decisions together? Could our 180-day-old relationship survive such a major shift?

After much coercion, I decided that it could. Besides, it wasn't my place to tell a grown man where he could and could not live.

But it was my place to say we shouldn't move in together. I insisted it was too soon when Alex suggested that we find a place of our own, so he moved in with a friend from Michigan who already had a two bedroom in the East Village. Those first few frigid weeks together were heaven. We bundled ourselves in giant jackets and drank martinis by the fireplace at the Waverly Inn. A lot of people hate New York in the winter, but it always makes me feel like I'm living in a Woody Allen movie. (The best time to be a New Yorker is when Christmas tourists have gone, but it's still cold and cozy.)

I had assumed Alex and I would spend a lot of time together at first. But as the weeks went by, I expected him to settle into a life of his own. Alex, however, struggled to find his way. My routines became his routines. My friends became his friends. My favorite places became his favorites too. All of this seemed natural and normal to a point—we were dating, and he had just moved here after a lifetime in another city. But as Alex remained unable to establish any connections or interests of his own, it started to seem like he had merely co-opted a life that I had spent years building. I started to resent him.

Since he had a roommate and I lived alone, Alex spent every night at my apartment. Never in my life have I yearned so desperately for a girls' night out. Even the idea of a solo trip to Equinox started to feel like an exotic vacation. (Naturally, Alex had also joined the same gym.) I began to spend exorbitant amounts of time in my bathtub, the only place where I could have some time to myself.

I was suffocating, but why, and how could I complain? Alex treated me so well. He was a great boyfriend. He anticipated my every need and was constantly doing thoughtful things, like showing up with my favorite pistachio macarons from Ladurée in Soho. How could I whine about my too-available boyfriend to friends who were hopelessly single? Or had just been dumped? Or were crying over the banker they met on Tinder who turned out to have a wife and two kids on the Upper West Side?

My mother was also in my head about Alex. Even though she was remarried to my stepfather—a wonderful man—she was still healing from my father's indiscretions. Her postdivorce mantra? Find a guy who loves you more than you love him. Alex seemed to be that guy. So I ignored my feelings, hunkered down, and decided to make things work.

Afraid of dumping the nicest guy on the planet, I was fine going along with Alex's and my new, shared life. Until I wasn't.

By the time August rolled around, I asked for a break from our relationship. Alex was devastated, questioning whether the separation had anything to do with an upcoming trip to Ibiza. (I hadn't invited Alex on the trip in an attempt to secure a week of independence for myself.) Somehow, I managed to convince both Alex and myself that the timing was just a "coincidence."

I could share so many stories about that trip to Ibiza, but I'm sure no one cares about my tequila-fueled tendencies or predilection for skinny-dipping. Instead, I'll focus on the highlights of being trapped on a Spanish island with two dozen single hotties. It was like a reality show.

We went clubbing every night. We slept during the day. I was a…less than good girl, even though I could assuage my guilt by telling myself Alex and I were on a break. (Was it possible that I was taking Ross's side and not Rachel's?)

None of the guys I fooled around with in Ibiza meant anything to me. They were like a fashion hair color—fun in the moment, but nothing to keep around long term. The rest of the crew became some of my best friends going forward. And by the time I boarded my first flight back to America, all I could think about was Alex. Maybe it was my throbbing hangover or the Guantanamo-like conditions of my EasyJet flight to London, but I would have traded every Chanel bag in my closet for one minute on the couch cuddling with Alex watching any romantic comedy. (Never mind the fact that Alex gamely watched all of my favorite chick flicks, which was part of the problem.)

We got back together.

Alex and I had some amazing moments over the next year and a half of our relationship. Moments when I could almost convince myself he was the one. Moments like when we traveled to India to see the sunrise over the Taj Mahal, or when I flew to Michigan to be present for the birth of his first niece. I told myself that I should stick with Alex, because no one would ever love me as much or as unconditionally as he did. But there's a big difference between loving someone and being in love with them. I think deep down I always knew he wasn't the one, but I ignored my gut.

I thought I was doing the right thing for both of us by staying. In reality, though, what I did was worse than a breakup. I dragged the poor guy along. By our final months together, I found myself craving attention from other men. The worse our relationship got, the sexier the photos I would post to my Instagram. I went out at

night with my girlfriends to flirt with other guys. I disrespected
Alex and am really not proud of it.

At some point I realized that all of my life I'd worried about the
guy cheating on me. But was Alex the one who should be worried?

There's only one thing I can say in self-defense: I was a twenty-
three-year-old girl. I had yet to explore my need for attention, my
fear of being alone. I hadn't met my life coach yet, who has been
transformative for me. It wasn't until I met her, Stacy, that I started
exploring my insecurities and working to repair them. Instead of
focusing on my past (even though it explained a lot of my insecurities) we focused on the present. "This is who you are, now let's
work on becoming the best version of yourself."

I may be an extremely confident woman when it comes to business. But when it came to love, I was always longing for the stability
of a boyfriend. Maybe it's because of my parents' failed marriage, or
maybe it's because I needed someone to ground me amid all the success from my blog. Whatever the reason, I kept making bad choices.

Alex put up with my behavior for a long time. But sometime
around his twenty-seventh birthday, he started to ask about the
next steps. We'd been dating for almost three years; he'd let me have
my fun, and now he needed to know if this was serious.

What did he want? To move in together. Something he'd been
pushing for since we first discussed his move to New York City.

I should have said no. But this was the first time in a long time
that Alex had showed any sort of backbone. It was just enough
of a display of confidence that I could convince myself he was

becoming the kind of guy that would challenge me. I accepted his offer and told myself that at least cohabitation would force me to decide once and for all whether this was my husband.

I realize now that living together should never be a test. There are a lot of reasons why New Yorkers move in with their significant other—the sky-high rents, the horrific subway system, how hard it is to find an Uber at 1:00 a.m. But the only *good* reason to cohabitate is if you think you're headed for marriage. Anything else is just a rationalization.

Alex and I found a two bedroom rental in the West Village. (Fun fact: It's the same apartment where I live—alone—today.) In typical Alex fashion, he suggested that we make the spare bedroom my wardrobe without me saying a word. *That's* how nice this guy was.

In an effort to create romance in our otherwise beige relationship, I took Alex to a seafood feast at The Clam on Hudson Street. Why not celebrate our first month of living together with a romantic dinner? And even though it's a bit of a cliché to consider oysters an aphrodisiac, they couldn't hurt? Right?

I donned a low-cut dress for the occasion. As we held hands over the candlelit table, I studied Alex's face and decided to ask if there were any activities that Alex had wanted to pursue now that we were living together. Now that he wasn't spending every night at someone else's apartment, he might want to take up a new hobby. *If he had something that he loved as much as I loved* WeWoreWhat, I thought, *we could reconnect again.*

"What do you mean a 'hobby'?" he asked, looking more handsome than ever in the Tom Ford button-down I had picked out for him.

"I don't know. I feel like you go straight from work, to me, back to work again. Isn't there something you want to do? Maybe something you used to enjoy as a kid? We have the space now for anything you want—an instrument, exercise equipment, you name it."

Alex considered my words. "Can't you be my hobby?" He thought he sounded cute—sexy even—but his answer was the exact problem.

"No, Alex. It can't." I let go of his hands and rubbed the goose bumps that had formed under my Isabel Marant dress. Was this conversation really happening? Could my handsome, intelligent twenty-seven-year-old boyfriend really not think of a single thing he'd like to do with his spare time?

He saw my face and tried to rectify the situation. "I like watching TV?"

"Alex. There has to be something in your life other than me, work, and TV."

I decided it wasn't going to work right then and there, midway through our uneaten crab cakes.

The next day, I flew to Paris for Fashion Week. I had mascara etched under my eyes from crying that wouldn't come off no matter how hard I scrubbed. We (and by that, I mean *I*) had decided that he would move his stuff out while I was overseas. Since Alex couldn't afford our apartment on his own, he would find a new place, and I would stay.

I continued to cry the entire seven hour flight to Charles de Gaulle. Once in Paris, I couldn't enjoy myself, even over dinner with foreign friends at Caviar Kaspia. I was too focused on and too distressed by the thought of Alex alone at home packing. I genuinely did (and still do) care for the guy, so much. Even if we weren't right together, I would never want to hurt him.

I desperately wanted to call Alex, to do anything that would make him feel better, but managed to stop myself. Everything I had done in an effort to be nice only seemed to make things worse. Perhaps the kindest thing I could do was leave him alone? It was time to give him some space. As for me, a second puppy seemed like a good idea. Introducing breakup dog number two, a French bulldog named Brooklyn.

Years later I've finally realized my well-meaning mom was wrong when she told me to stay with Alex. A woman isn't supposed to find a man who loves her more than she loves him. The trick is to find someone who is your equal. Someone who challenges you, someone you respect and can learn from. Everyone deserves to find someone whom they not only love, but are also in love *with*.

And when I do manage to find that person…well, I'll never, ever let them go.

Vet Your Business Partners like Your Romantic Ones

I've come to realize that picking business partners is no less difficult or important than picking romantic ones. The best relationships are with those you click with but who are also truthful and transparent. If you feel like someone is being dishonest…well, then you should trust your gut and confront the situation. When you're dating, this type of behavior protects your heart. But when it comes to business, it protects your *brand*.

Around the time I hit five hundred thousand followers, my value to advertisers seemed to solidify. The requests were pouring in. But still, I wasn't satisfied. I yearned for the kind of deeper partnerships that allowed me to go beyond some simple styling tips and a sponsored photo. I was an opinionated woman with an eye for fashion. Surely, brands would start to take notice.

And they did! Soon, advertisers started seeing me as more than just a marketing vehicle. A few even wanted me to create my own capsule collections under their brand—essentially becoming the designer Grandma Joyce had hoped I would be ever since she gave me that sewing machine back in high school. The advantage to me was obvious: I could design without having to create my own brand and infrastructure. Partnering with an existing brand that could help my designs come to life seemed like the obvious way to start. I could dip my toes into designing without any risk.

My first big design collaboration was a collection for Topshop, a brand that I worked with frequently and whose London Fashion Week shows I had attended many times (during which I was paid to post on social media). Topshop had noticed how well my posts converted to sales and understood the value of my reach. Also, next to New York, my strongest following was in London, where they were headquartered and had their biggest retail stores.

The collab would be for jewelry, and the goal was to start small and tell a story too. Topshop wasn't totally confident in my ability to design my own jewelry line (and why should they be? I'd never done anything like it). To offset my greenness, they felt it best to offer me some inspiration—and where better to be inspired than the Grand Bazaar in Istanbul, considered by many to be the greatest jewelry flea market on the planet? Surely there would be enough vintage pieces there to get my creative juices flowing.

An overpacker since birth, I stared at my suitcase for hours before deciding what to bring. Even though I plan every outfit in advance (then take pictures so I won't forget how I want to style them), I still bring extra options in case the weather changes or, more likely, my mood. I have always firmly believed that more is more when it comes to packing. So what if you have to wait in baggage claim upon arrival? It's worth it to have everything you need. (I've been told my issue is how I define the word "need" in this context, but whatever.) Plus, Topshop said I could pull whatever I wanted from their latest season to wear on the trip. #swoon

I arrived in Istanbul, suitcases full of Topshop in tow, and headed up to my room for a much-needed shower. The hotel was beautiful, and so naturally the first thing I did was post my sweet new digs. When I left the hotel for dinner later, there were eight Turkish girls lined up out front. "I can't believe it's really you," one of them yelled as she demanded a selfie. "We are your *biggest* fans in Turkey. We've been waiting here all day just so we could meet you." I have a lot of great memories from that trip, but this one was special because it was the first time I realized just how global my brand was. I'm always taken aback when a fan approaches me, but that experience (in Turkey, of all places!) truly left me stunned and humbled.

Needless to say, Topshop was a great partner. The collab was a major success and gave me the confidence to pursue similar partnerships. *Almost* all of the brands that I've worked with during my decade-long career as an influencer have been great. There was one collaboration, however, that was anything but a fairy tale. In retrospect, it was a straight-up mistake.

In the summer of 2015, I had plans to fly to Chicago for the Lollapalooza music festival. I called in samples from dozens of brands—clothes that I could bring with me but, sadly, would have to be returned after the trip. (Despite popular belief, I don't get to keep everything that I wear.) But no matter how hard I looked, I found myself missing one item: the perfect pair of black booties—a pair that somehow didn't manage to exist in my *extremely* comprehensive collection. Everything I owned either cut my calf in a weird place or had a toe that was just a little too round. I scoured the sites of Shopbop and Net-a-Porter, willing to pay whatever it took, but still came up empty-handed.

At the time, I was peripheral friends with a man named Seth who owned a made-to-order shoe company headquartered near Penn Station. We had met once upon a time at Fashion Week— during an event at a now-deceased club called Fat Baby. Side note: New York is like a revolving door for clubs and restaurants. What's cool one day is lame the next. Once a hotspot gets too much press, it scares off the who's who of New York. It's a catch-22 for influencers, whose job it is to post but who want to keep their favorite places under the radar. But I've learned to stop posting after my second drink of the night.

All this to say, Fat Baby was still hot when Seth and I met there.

Seth was the kind of New York guy we all meet at some point in our twenties. He was old and suave enough to convince fashion newcomers that he was sophisticated, but too young and tasteless to be accepted by the establishment. He might have a few photos in celebrity photographer Patrick McMullan's archive, but Anna Wintour wouldn't give this guy a second glance. (Something a guy like him will always insist doesn't bother him, even though it keeps him up at night.)

I, however, didn't have the good sense or wherewithal then that I have today. I thought Seth was someone to emulate. He always let me borrow shoes and even let me borrow the photo studio in his office whenever I had a shoot. I looked past his odd attachment to fedoras to the good guy I thought he was.

When I told Seth about my Lollapalooza boot-tastrophe, and that I had been unable to find a solution in his existing line of SKUs, he offered to create my dream festival shoe. Keep in mind, his company was made-to-order, which gave them the flexibility to manufacture one-off designs right in the middle of New York City.

Together, we walked through his midtown factory with Seth listening as I shouted out opinions on his current collection. "I like this one, but the shaft is too high." "This one needs a pointier, but not too pointy, toe." One nice thing I can say about Seth is that he was open to my design direction.

Three weeks later I was in possession of the world's most perfect Chelsea boot, complete with embroidered silver stars on the heel. All Seth demanded in return? For me to tag his brand when I wore them, which I was more than happy to do.

The day after I posted those boots—their heels sinking into the muddy grounds of Chicago's Grant Park—Seth's company was flooded with requests from curious customers. *What are these?*

Where can I get them? I can't find them on your website! Even big brands like Free People and Revolve were asking how they could stock them. (I, too, received more than a few direct messages asking how to get the boots.)

Seth called me the next day to discuss launching a line together. Clearly the demand for my designs was there; all Seth had to do was manufacture and distribute them. As soon as I got back to New York, we sat down with Seth's chief financial officer and my firecracker agent, Jen Powell. (Jen had recently left the company she worked for, Next Models, to become an independent powerhouse. Her goal that day was to figure out how *We Wore What* could monetize all the excitement from my Chelsea boots.)

It was clear that this was going to be a very different type of partnership than what I had with Topshop and other brands. For one, Seth's business was a lot smaller, which meant this was going to require a lot more hustle on my part. What we decided to do was essentially create a standalone brand—with its own identity, name, and website—under Seth's existing company.

Seth wanted to call the line "*We Wore What* Shoes," or something similar that would profit off my rising notoriety. I, however, was adamant that this new enterprise be a distinct business with its own name. I remember being worried that my brand name wasn't big enough to bring in the necessary sales yet.

I also wanted to keep growing *We Wore What* as a lifestyle platform before I launched any branded products. Sure, I had learned a lot about designing for other brands. But I had no idea how to create, manufacture, and distribute a product without that kind of infrastructure. There was a lot to learn, and I wanted to learn without risking my namesake. I always knew I would launch *WeWoreWhat* designs, but wasn't ready to use my one shot.

In the end, we named the brand Archive Shoes after the West Village apartment building where I lived prior to moving in with Alex.

Archive Shoes's first release was epic. I designed a collection of the five most perfect boots—the boots a girl wanted to live in but could never seem to find. They were classic, high quality, and chic. Of course we released a Chelsea boot because of the previous excitement, but I also added in a thigh-high, a glove bootie, a biker boot, and a high-heeled bootie.

Sure, I did all the normal things designers do. I pulled inspiration from magazines, vintage photos, and street style imagery. More than that, though, I referenced my own incredibly full closet. (I had the added benefit of being sent gifted shoes from just about every brand on the planet.) If there was a boot that I wanted and didn't already own, then it was safe to say it didn't exist in the market.

As I looked through my collection, I came to a realization: each pair had elements that I liked, but none were perfect. What if I could combine different aspects to make one *mega*boot?

It took three months to create that first line. Initial sketches were done by me personally, and then I worked closely with Seth's team to bring my designs to life. I visited their midtown office at least twice a week to participate in meetings, look at leather samples, and help select details like sole shape and hardware. I was deeply involved in every step of the process, from heel to toe.

Since our first line was direct-to-consumer, we launched on a new Archive Shoes website and sold the boots there alone. Within a week, Seth and I had practically sold out of our inventory. Retailers like Shopbop and Revolve were reaching out to ask about stocking any future collections. It was an undeniable success.

Obviously, Seth and I wanted to create another collection together—Seth because Archive Shoes was already profitable, and me because I was having so much fun designing footwear. I decided to reinvest my entire portion of revenue from our first line into our second to fund the production and new hires who would be responsible for press and wholesale.

Since my first collection had focused on classic boots, I decided to have a little more fun with the second round of designs. This time I gravitated toward stylized looks, like buckled combat boots and lace-up kitten heels. They were still superwearable but more fashion forward than what I had designed before. I couldn't wait for the first samples to arrive from the factory so I could see them in real life.

So what was the first thing I realized when the samples finally did arrive? That the quality seemed off. The leather felt less expensive, the sole was a different rubber, the laces felt cheap. I may not have been a production guru, but it didn't take a rocket scientist to see that corners were being cut.

In typical Danielle fashion, I confronted Seth right away. He explained that he had moved production from Italy to China in order to maximize profit margins but promised that the boots would still wear well. When I asked why he hadn't consulted me, Seth spun some bullshit about me being new to manufacturing and not wanting to weigh down my creativity with nitty gritty business details. It should have been concerning, but I was honestly too inexperienced to know what was normal.

I pressed Seth for more information. *What were the specifics around our sales on the first collection? More importantly, what were our costs of production? If the second collection was cheaper to manufacture, could we lower the price from $350 to $280?* Seth would always give me these roundabout answers. He would send a spreadsheet with impressive sales numbers, but I couldn't seem to get direct access to the Archive Shoes Shopify account that held all of our back-end data. I don't recall ever seeing production costs or what items were being returned.

I was starting to get a bad taste in my mouth but was already deep in designs for our third collection—a spring line of loafers and sandals that you can still see on the Archive Shoes website to this day. I had just finished a third round of designs when the second collection was hitting the market. That's when my Instagram account was flooded with angry messages from customers complaining about broken zippers, lost shipments, and long wait times. It was the opposite of what I wanted for my brand.

I met with Seth to complain and express my serious disappointment. My reputation was on the line. He claimed innocence, explaining that these kind of issues are natural when creating a new brand, but something felt off. I started to remember all the other warning signs I had ignored throughout Seth's and my friendship.

I should have known better. I'd seen him be rude to not only his employees, but also to me. He literally yelled at me in front of my employees on more than one occasion. He was frequently late to meetings and was an infamous partier. He ignored most of my emails for days on end. And yet I still had gone into business with him.

I called my attorney and told her I wanted out.

Fortunately, I have always been extremely cautious about contracts and owned the Archive Shoes trademark outright. It would be illegal for Seth to continue the line without me. I closed the Archive Shoes Instagram and made a public announcement that the brand would be shutting down due to unforeseen circumstances. (Thank God I had refused to name the line after my blog.)

I'll never know how much money we made on the second collection. I could see how many pieces had sold, but I wasn't seeing all our expenses—how much money had actually been made once we were done manufacturing and distributing the shoes. That means I didn't know our net profits, which is basically the only number that mattered.

Seth never paid me for the second collection ; the third collection was never made (to my knowledge). And since I reinvested my portion of the first collection into the company, I never made a single dollar from Archive Shoes. In the end, I decided to keep this story quiet (until now). To view the whole thing as a very painful, expensive lesson. A legal battle and ensuing publicity shitstorm wasn't worth the money. In my opinion, getting lawyers involved to sue will almost always end up costing you more money than you gain.

I made so many mistakes in this venture. Sure, I knew and liked Seth socially (at first), but I should have done more research before I agreed to go into business with him. I should have talked to people who had worked with him to make sure our morals were in alignment. I should have been smarter about picking my partner.

So how do I operate differently today? Now I make sure my contracts give me full control every step of the way—especially when it comes to questions about quality. I add legal language that demands full transparency on everything from the cost of manufacturing to decisions around wholesale pricing. I make sure I legally have creative say over my designs and branding. Everything from who does the press, to who gets free shoes, to how we respond to customers...it's all approved by me.

But unfortunately, no matter how much research you do, the people you work with can always surprise you. There is no way of protecting yourself one hundred percent. That's why it's so important to think long and hard before partnering with someone. How to say no to money is one of the hardest things I've had to learn, but it's the only way to remain authentic and protect my brand.

Never Let Love Blind You

Okay, I have to admit. I haven't been entirely honest with you guys. Most of what I told you about my relationship with Alex is true, but there *was* more to the story.

Alex moved out of our apartment in early 2017, right around the time I shuttered Archive Shoes. Rather than sever things completely, however, we decided to keep seeing each other on a more casual basis. I helped him find his own place just down the block from our—I mean, my—apartment. But I also started dating other guys. (I told Alex he could do the same but was safe in the assumption that he never would.)

I knew it was wrong, but I was too comfortable, scared, and immature to cut Alex off completely. The thought of being alone was terrifying. A lot of people think success makes it easier to be single, but I think it's actually harder for a myriad reasons that I won't get into. I wanted to have my cake and eat it, too, unable to let Alex go completely while still being open to meeting someone new.

Two months into our new arrangement, I flew to Palm Springs on a sponsored trip to Coachella. While at the music festival, I found myself chatting with a peripheral influencer friend and her new husband. Drunkenly, I spilled the details of my current predicament: that I was dating the nicest guy in the world—whom most girls would kill to marry—and yet I wanted nothing to do with him.

When the happy couple asked what was missing, I explained that I was yearning for a challenge. Someone as amazing as Alex but still strong enough to put me in my place. Unfortunately, those guys usually turned out to be dicks.

That's when I saw the newlyweds exchange a conspiratorial glance. "We have *just* the guy for you," my friend said. "He's kind of an asshole, but you might like him."

Color me intrigued.

They gave me his number and told me to call when I got back to New York. But there had been too much tequila, and I decided to FaceTime him right then and there—literally from the VIP section of the Lumineers concert. He answered, groggy, and curtly explained that he had been sleeping. Not just because of the three-hour time difference, but also because he was a thirty-five-year-old man. (And therefore no longer considered Thursday night part of the weekend.)

His name was Rob. We agreed to go out the following week.

Of course, what had seemed like a good idea when I was three thousand miles away in California felt terrifying once I was back in the city (and reimmersed in the Alex/Danielle drama). I panicked and decided to call off the date.

Then he called, mere minutes after my red-eye landed on Monday morning. It was an unusual move for 2017, when most guys communicated via text. Rob, however, was old school—something I appreciated.

"I'm so sorry, but I don't think we should see each other," I told him as I walked up the jet bridge. I tried to remain firm, even as my body lit up at the sound of his voice.

"Why? Do you have a boyfriend?" He got everything he needed from my silence.

"I do. But it was really nice to meet you, and I wish you the best." And then I hung up.

I tried so hard to be good. I went weeks without contacting Rob, even though I thought about him constantly. But there's this bar on the Lower East Side of Manhattan called Flower Shop that has a tendency to take all your best efforts toward morality and tell them to go fuck themselves. Flower Shop wants you to be *bad*.

I met my friend Tara there the night before I was about to fly to Morocco for a wedding. Shots were had. A white silk Reformation dress was worn with fishnets peeking through. And at one point in the evening, I don't remember when or why, I texted Rob. If he wanted to meet me, well, this was his chance. I was off to Africa the next day.

Keep in mind that I knew next to nothing about Rob. We'd never met. We had no mutual friends other than that couple at Coachella. We had only spoken twice on the phone. But there was something about this guy…a chemistry so electric that it didn't require physical contact.

Rob arrived at Flower Shop thirty minutes later, sporting that season's Saint Laurent Chelsea boot with a black Henley and a leather jacket. Tara stuck around just long enough to make sure he wasn't a serial killer, then slipped away without farewells. That I allowed myself to be alone with Rob before things were fully done with Alex was my first (or fiftieth) mistake.

In my pathetic defense, Rob knew I was still involved with Alex. I told him everything that night. He listened to my story with a level of focus that I'd yet to receive from any guys my age. Then, he gave me sound advice: either stop fucking around and give Alex a real chance, or let him go forever.

"The worst part about what you're doing is preventing this poor guy from moving on," Rob explained.

He was right. I took a moment to contemplate his wisdom—which must be a symptom of his older age—and then, confusingly, he kissed me. The kind of kiss that makes every extremity tingle. From there, I let myself get carried away.

I called Rob the next day to suggest that last night had been a mistake. (A fun mistake, but a mistake all the same.) Rob suggested that we just be friends until things were fully over with Alex. Was this maturity? If it was, it was pretty attractive.

In Morocco, the distance gave me some much-needed time for introspection. I was able to spend the trip celebrating my friend's marriage and contemplating my life back in Manhattan. Should I stay with Alex, whom I didn't love but who would also never hurt me? Or should I take a risk and pursue Rob, who was so unlike anyone I had ever met before?

When I got home, I ended things with Alex—for real this time. (Naturally, I stayed mum on the Rob topic and focused on the issues with our relationship.) I decided not to tell Rob I was officially single but reinitiated our "friendship" while I gave myself some time to heal. The two of us fell into the habit of talking multiple times a day—always on the phone, never over text.

It seemed to be going well, until a few weeks later when Rob called with a more serious tone. "Listen, it's no secret that I have feelings for you," he said. "I know you just got out of a serious relationship, but I can't just be your friend. So why don't you take some time to think about what you want and get back to me?"

I didn't need to think about it. I decided to make a grand gesture and show up at Rob's place unannounced, where I would tell him I wanted to be together. He wasn't in the city but had moved into his house in the Hamptons that he had gotten all on his own. (I remember thinking that kind of independence was so sexy when he first told me about it.)

I marched up to Rob's house and knocked, my bags (hopefully) packed for me to be able to stay. Seconds later the door flew open to reveal Rob, still shirtless from his morning run. He blinked furiously, as if he couldn't believe his eyes.

"Danielle? What are you doing here?" he asked, incredulous.

"I don't need time to think," I said, taking a step closer. "I want to try this."

Rob averted his gaze to the sky, deep in thought. I froze. Had I misread the entire situation? Was this *not* what Rob wanted?

Then…he kissed me for the first time since that night at Flower Shop weeks earlier. I never wanted the moment to end. He picked me up like a bride crossing the threshold and carried me straight to his bedroom.

After that day, I threw myself into Rob like I throw my credit card into a Bottega sample sale—passionately and without consideration of the future. There was one obvious issue: Rob, at thirty-five years old, was ten years my senior. It was a pretty significant age gap.

I spent every weekend for the rest of the summer with Rob in the Hamptons. We had great sex. He cooked amazing dinners using ingredients we'd bought at the local farmers market. He took me to watch a seemingly endless number of sunsets on the Peconic Bay. I tried to play it cool, but it was hopeless. I was obsessed. After spending my entire life dating boys, I had finally found a man.

The summer flew by like a fairy tale. But was it all too good to be true? I wouldn't know if this was for real until we were back in the city. Only once we were back to real life would I know for sure that this wasn't a holiday romance.

And then one day we were walking into the movie theater on a rainy afternoon in Sag Harbor, because why else would you go to the movies in the Hamptons except for a storm? It's a tiny, decades-old place with stale popcorn and a single screen. Rob and I were waiting to buy off-brand concessions when we ran into two of his friends—friends to whom he introduced me as his *girlfriend*, Danielle.

We were officially dating.

The summer was going so well—until a Friday morning at the end of August, when my mom called with terrible news. My grandfather, Poppy Ivan, had been battling pancreatic cancer for months. The illness had come on suddenly at eighty-six years old. One day, he was working on his swing at the golf course. The next day, he was bedridden.

Poppy's diagnosis had rocked all of our lives. And now, according to his nurse, he was dying. If I wanted to say goodbye, I needed to rush to the hospice center. Right. Now. There wasn't much time.

As I had grown up only a few blocks away from my grandparents, Poppy Ivan was like a second father to me. He had worked in retail back in the day and was the only member of my family who even vaguely understood the fashion industry. He would even drive me to the train every morning when I was interning in the city, always with a toasted bagel waiting for me in the passenger seat of his Lincoln, telling me all the ways that I was his "little prodigy." So, even though I had time to internalize his cancer diagnosis, I wasn't prepared to say goodbye to such an important fixture in my life.

Rob sped the entire way there and then waited in the car. He didn't want to come inside and intrude, but he did want to be close in case I needed him. When it came time for the shiva, he spent hours sitting with us (which couldn't have been an easy first way to meet my family). It was then that I started to think this could really be something. Maybe, just maybe, I had found my person.

Cut to eighteen months later: I had not found my person.

In retrospect, it's obvious how Rob was not the guy for me. He was sexy, he was older, he appeared to have his shit together. But appearances can be deceiving, especially if you keep your eyes shut and ignore the warning signs.

Rather than blabber on and on about what went wrong with Rob—which would bore you guys and tear me apart—I'll just distill our almost-two-year relationship into a list of red flags I now watch for when considering potential partners. If your suitor exhibits even one of these behaviors…well, then it might be time to cut bait.

1. **I made too many excuses for him.** Rob was extremely close to his family. Considering that, one would imagine he would also want to be close to mine. In reality, though, Rob skipped almost every Bernstein event while we were together. I made so many excuses for him—*He has to work* or *He isn't feeling well*. Meanwhile I chose to focus on who Rob had been at the start

of our relationship—the Rob who dropped everything to take me to Poppy Ivan. I spent months telling myself *that* was the real Rob. Never again will I date someone who requires so many excuses.

2. **He avoided my friends.** Rob didn't just avoid my family; he also avoided my friends. The reason? Rob considered my gang "young" and "silly." When Rob *did* spend time with my friends, he would shit-talk them for days after. We had always talked about how our age difference might impact our relationship, but Rob insisted that I wasn't "a normal twenty-five-year-old." (This should have been a sign, but all I felt was pride at being "mature for my age.") I let him drive a wedge between me and my friends, and it was stupid.

3. **His criticism wasn't constructive.** One of the things that first attracted me to Rob was how much he cared about *WeWoreWhat*. Not only did I have this older, wiser boyfriend, but he was also willing to lend his business expertise to help the company grow. He was almost an adviser in the sense that we would spend hours during

what was meant to be a romantic dinner at Nobu discussing how to boost company profits. (It actually *was* really romantic that he cared.)

But the longer we dated, the more Rob's constructive criticism devolved into *criticism*. He would call certain brands too "lowbrow" for me to work with. He thought influencer trips were "stupid." And don't even get me started on what it was like when we vacationed as a couple…he would give me a hard time about taking a *single* photo of me, even though we were getting the trip for free in exchange for me posting. I *almost* started to believe him, *almost* became embarrassed over my job, *almost* rethought the brand's longevity. It was a dark time.

4. **He was controlling.** After a year together, Rob started to complain about certain photos on my Instagram feed. He specifically hated bikini shots, which is hilarious considering that my swim line launched during our relationship. Soon, I was seeking Rob's permission before posting any photo that was even vaguely sexual. It was the only way to keep from arguing.

Every decision from where we ate dinner to the brand of apple cider vinegar in my fridge was subject to Rob's opinion. (The guy was really particular about his apple cider vinegar.) Because in Rob's mind, he always knew best— even though I was the only one of us who had started a multimillion dollar company. But I digress. I am *not* the kind of person who bows down to men, so it was incredibly disconcerting to see myself doing so for Rob. I lost myself, my strength, the second I gave someone else control over my emotions.

5. **He didn't show up.** I never asked Rob to attend industry events. The one time I did, it was for a black tie gala. I was beyond drained—having spent the prior week schlepping all over the city for New York Fashion Week—and needed him there for emotional support. The event took place on a Saturday, but Rob refused to go and spent the night with his friends instead. My mom had to step in at the last minute as my plus one. This is just one example of an ongoing theme in which Rob almost never showed up for me—at least not after the honeymoon period. It was no good.

I can tell myself I didn't notice any of these red flags until after Rob and I broke up, but the truth is that I noticed several early on. I ignored my gut because I was so in love—blind and powerless to my emotions. Whether I was so obsessed with him or with the idea of him, I'll never know.

It would take two breakups before Rob and I ended things for good. The first separation devastated me. Unable to eat, I lost ten pounds. I spent hours with my life coach, telling her how lost I was without the relationship. I have always been so confident and self-assured that I hadn't even noticed myself drifting away.

Stacy explained that there was work to be done. I needed to learn how to be alone—*happily*—before I could consider dating again. So how would I start learning to love Danielle again? By forgiving myself for all the mistakes I'd made during my last two relationships.

I did the work. I took a break from men and decided not to have another boyfriend again until I stopped feeling like I needed one. I focused on self-love. Now I knew that I had to be strong on my own before I could add someone else to the picture. Finally, I thought I was healed.

But clearly I wasn't…because Rob and I got back together.

Our relationship was really good at first. Rob turned back into the man he'd been at the start of our relationship, promising things would be different. After only a few weeks, though, it turned back to shit. He avoided my friends. He continued to chastise my "meaningless" career as an influencer. He promised to be better after every fight, but he never was.

In November 2018, Rob broke up with me. Again. I told him this was the *last* time. There would be no more teary reunions. We were done. For good.

"We are never ever, ever, ever getting back together," I screamed, unaware that I was quoting Taylor Swift. "I won't be here next time you come crawling back."

Despite my anger, this breakup was just as devastating as the last one. But at least I knew it was for the best. It had taken almost two years, but I finally realized that you can't change people. The only person you can change is yourself. That's why I decided that I needed to do more work on me—to relearn self-respect.

Part of my journey toward emotional health also involved improving myself physically. Enter Melissa Wood, the kind of person who exudes enough energy and positivity to attract anyone. She's also a certified health and wellness coach who specializes in a unique combination of movement, meditation, and mindful eating. We were introduced by a mutual friend around the time that I was dating Rob. I remember her saying, "I don't like the way you're talking about your body. Let's work out together sometime."

It messes with your head to share pictures of yourself with millions of people—strangers who often want to criticize—each day. Add on a reproving boyfriend, and you're in danger of some serious insecurity. I wasn't self-conscious about my weight growing up, but had become that way in my twenties. I grew obsessed with photo editing tools that I could use to make my thighs a little thinner or arms a little more sculpted. Between the exposure and slew of drama-filled relationships, I started to feel like the real me just wasn't good enough. Putting myself in front of two million people every day was my choice, but that didn't make it easy. Hateful comments would come at me from all different angles, publicly and through my private messages. I grew a thick skin, but sometimes it just wasn't enough.

After my breakup with Rob I was at a low point, and something had to be done. I started seeing both Stacy and Melissa on a weekly basis. I took up Pilates and meditation. I felt calmer, more confident, and (best of all) happier with myself. Melissa taught me about food combining, that "diet" is a dirty word, how to get long, lean lines, and how to have a different perspective when it comes to working out and eating well. With Stacy, we worked on my mental state. She forced me to look deeper and question my responsibility in how I behaved and how I kept repeating bad habits. Both Melissa and Stacy changed my life; they saved me, and I owe a lot to them.

In the end, Rob dumping me was one of the best things that ever happened because it prompted me to change both my life and the way I present myself on social media. Fewer filters, more transparency. I try to be nicer to myself, both mentally and physically.

Rob taught me to never let love blind you, to look out for the red flags early on. And if you find yourself making excuses for your partner's behavior, run. But there is one lesson that I took from Rob's and my relationship that I hold above all else: that the most important relationship is the one you have with yourself. It's my life motto. To be happy with *me*. And how could I find that happiness? By working to become the woman I'd once been—toward the woman I hoped to be and would want to share with the world.

LESSON TWENTY-ONE

Execution Is Everything

I love overalls. Hence why my blog's first tagline was "Overalls are my second skin." I don't know when my obsession started, but one-pieces have always felt like the perfect, hassle-free outfit. Plus, they never go out of style. They are the George Clooney of fashion.

There's just one tiny problem with overalls. (And I'm not talking about how hard it is to pee while wearing them.) Finding a great pair is about as difficult as finding a Jewish doctor who lives below Fourteenth Street and maintains an appropriate relationship with his mother—a.k.a. *impossible.*

Denim fit is always complicated, but especially when it comes to overalls. I used to order dozens of pairs off the internet, only to find them misshapen or of poor quality. Either the fabric was too stiff or too thin; they rode too high or too low. The bib shape was either too big or too small. I felt like the Goldilocks of overalls, always searching for her perfect pair.

Despite the absence of good overalls on the market, I still managed to accumulate a pretty killer collection over the years. People would always ask where I got them, ready to ditch whatever party we were at and sprint to the store. In reality, though, the only pairs I wore were vintage. (For unknown reasons the entire world stopped making great overalls after 1985.) I was way more likely to find options at Metropolis Vintage than I was at Barney's. For those who can't bear the smell or time required for secondhand shopping, finding a great pair of overalls seemed impossible.

At one point I was having an ongoing conversation with my lead adviser, my father, about the future of *WeWoreWhat*. He was always looking for ways I could transition my following into something "tangible," as he would say.

"When you look back at the last few years, Danielle, what part of your job have you enjoyed the most?" I remember him asking over a dozen Wellfleets at the Grand Central Oyster Bar.

"I really like creating my own products," I replied, thinking about how much I'd enjoyed designing that line for Archive Shoes, despite all the headaches. "Maybe I'd like to have my own label someday."

"Well, whatever you design, think long and hard about your first product. Make sure it's something you know intimately. Something you use in your day-to-day life. That way you'll know you can do it better than anyone else."

That was great advice. And better yet, it made the product that I should design seem so obvious. Overalls! Not only did I wear them all the time, but I also knew there was a demand and a need for better options. There was no one brand that made awesome, well-fitting, quality overalls. I could fill an empty space in the market and have a niche brand.

Keep in mind, I was a college dropout with only one employee at the time. (Hey, Moe.) There was no world in which I could compete with big brands like Levi's and Rag & Bone. The denim industry is *so* saturated. There are more companies than I can count, and I didn't want to upset the brands who were also paying me to work with them.

I decided the smartest way to go about things was to take my dad's advice and start with a single product: overalls. If I focused on this one item, then I could make it better than anyone else. Create something so easy and wearable that it would be impossible not to buy.

A week later, I met up with a PR friend of mine named Elizabeth Tuke. Not only does Elizabeth run her own firm, Tuke Consulting, but she's also a fashion insider on Meghan Markle's speed dial. Sure, she's so short that she barely comes up to my belly button. But she packs more oomph into that five-feet-two frame than I ever thought possible. She's awesome, to say the least.

We met for paninis at the Sant Ambroeus on West Fourth Street. Elizabeth arrived in her usual Upper East Side garb, a stark contrast to the tattered jeans I donned for the occasion. (The woman only wears designer dresses. I don't think I've ever seen her in a pair of pants, except for our overalls on launch day.)

The meeting was purely social. We were happily knocking back cappuccinos when she asked what I was up to, and I decided to tell Elizabeth my new idea.

I lowered my voice. "I'm interested in launching a company," I said. "A line that would consist solely of overalls. I don't know. Is that crazy?"

"No, I love that!" Her eyes lit up, and she stopped playing with the Harry Winston pearls around her neck. "Do you want a partner? You could handle the designs; I could run the PR."

I can always count on Elizabeth to cut the shit and get straight to the point. Like I said, the girl is short but scrappy AF.

The decision was a no brainer. Elizabeth was the perfect choice—not just because she knows the PR business, but also because she's a female entrepreneur with her own company. She knows how to start something from scratch. (I also genuinely like her and was happy for an excuse to spend significant amounts of time together.)

We decided to call the line Second Skin Overalls, or SSO for short, an homage to my blog's original tagline, "Overalls are my second skin." Our first hire was a (very expensive) freelance denim expert named Monique, who had the perfect résumé with experience at both J. Crew and Gap. As soon as we found her, Elizabeth and I plowed full steam ahead on bringing our first collection to life. (I tend to jump into things right away. People spend a lot of time talking about their ideas, but execution is everything. We need to stop thinking and just *do*.)

To mimic the initial success we'd had with Archive Shoes, I decided to start with a line of five classic overalls that focused on quality and fit. We called the collection "The Basics," including the high rise skinny, the '70s jumpsuit, the high rise flare, the relaxed fit, and the oversized culotte.

I knew I didn't want to take on any outside investments. Taking someone's money means you're forfeiting a piece of your company and, in most situations, control. But if I was going to fund the entire process myself, which I did, it meant we were going to have to bootstrap. There would be no budget for anything extraneous. We needed to keep as much of the work in-house as possible—which meant that Elizabeth and I had a lot to learn about the ins and outs of production.

We built the entire company, soup to nuts. Elizabeth focused on finding a freelance programmer to build our website. Moe jumped in to tour dozens of New Jersey warehouses until she found the perfect company to handle shipping and fulfillment. I not only designed the overalls but also produced and starred in all of our marketing materials. It was more work than we could have ever predicted.

Monique's job was to coordinate with factories around the production of our overalls. And since most of her existing connections were in China, it was a foregone conclusion that we would manufacture in Asia—considered the least expensive, but also the slowest, option. At the time, we were happy to pursue price over speed. I had yet to even announce that I was releasing a line of overalls. No one would notice if it took a few months longer than anticipated.

Four months and $100,000 of my own savings later, SSO was ready to launch. The overalls looked and felt flawless. I, however, was a bundle of nerves. I had spent years proving my ability to generate sales for established brands like Zimermann or Topshop. But would that translate to my own initiatives? We were about to find out.

My fears were assuaged when Second Skin Overalls sold $70,000 worth of product in the first hour. By the end of that day, we were sold out. That's *before* Bella Hadid and Emily Ratajkowski ever posted themselves wearing my designs.

I was flooded with validation. It's difficult to explain, but a part of me had been in as much doubt about the power of influencers as the rest of the world. I lived with a deep sense of imposter syndrome. Did I really deserve these massive paychecks? And even if I did at the moment, couldn't it all go away tomorrow? But then here was this brand that I had designed, created, and marketed myself, and we were already operating on a months-long waitlist. I put the proof in my own goddamn pudding, and it was a dream come true.

That's the good news. The bad news is that I made so many mistakes when launching Second Skin—mistakes I want to help everyone else avoid. Below are my top errors broken into bullet points. It's not an entirely inclusive list, but it does contain the most valuable lessons I took away from the first line of SSO.

1. **Be careful whom you trust.** I trusted too many people and grew my team too quickly. One employee stole my designs and sold them to other factories overseas. Another lied about the cost of a fabric order so that she could pocket extra cash for herself. These mistakes could have been avoided if my books had been in order, but they weren't. As a result we weren't profitable until our third collection.

2. **Find the right warehouse.** We changed shipping partners multiple times at the beginning of SSO. There were also constant issues with fulfillment. Either goods would be damaged upon arrival, or orders would disappear in transit, or customers would complain about orders not arriving on time. I was constantly looking for a new warehouse, which was a drain both emotionally and financially.

3. **Find the right factory.** Ditto everything I said about shipping partners, except even more

important. Focus on ethics and quality, transparency, and efficiency.

4. **Trademark your brand's name.** This should be the first thing you ever do when starting a new company. I never even thought to trademark the name Second Skin Overalls, which turned out to be owned by Dick's Sporting Goods. One cease and desist order later, I was rebranding the entire brand to SSO by Danielle.

5. **Don't try to do everything yourself.** At first, I tried to micromanage the entire operation. But the production process was a fresh hell for me—an area in which I had no experience. So when you finally *do* find the right partners, you have to stop withholding your trust and let them do their things. Stick to what you do best, and let the experts take over. That's why you hired them.

The biggest problem was that these mistakes slowed us down. Modern shoppers want instant gratification and new arrivals all the time. They forget about you the second you're not in front of them. (Hence why brands like Supreme are always dropping new and exclusive products.) So if it takes six months to release a new collection instead of the planned three…well, that's a problem.

Still, the brand was a success. We released five collections as Second Skin Overalls, and grossed hundreds of thousands of dollars, all while staying direct-to-consumer (which means we were only available through our own website; no one else could carry our products). Making a conscious effort to keep demand high, we continued to release small but frequent drops with only a modest amount of product.

And perhaps most important, we decided to keep customer service in-house. There are a ton of third party vendors whom you can hire to run customer service. I, however, have always known that I wanted to be in control of that feedback—to let it dictate the progression of the company. Every email sent was read by either me or Moe, and that kept us close to our consumers.

Major department stores quickly approached Elizabeth and me about buying the brand, but we didn't bite…because there was a larger plan. It wasn't until August 2019 that I decided to close Second Skin Overalls and relaunch as WeWoreWhat Overalls with an existing brand (Onia) as my production partner. More on that later.

What I learned from the early years of SSO was not to beat myself up over mistakes. Sure, they happen. They can even feel devastating. But it's not the error that matters. It's what you do next—how you grow—that defines who you are as an entrepreneur. I had just learned that same message from my relationship with Rob, but now I was learning it again when it came to business. I can finally tell the universe it's beating a dead horse—I get the point. Mistakes are going to happen, and that's okay because they will make me smarter and stronger.

A Twist of Fate

One of the best parts of my job is that I get to travel the world to work with different brand partners. Sometimes we call these influencer trips, and they usually look pretty glamorous to our followers (which most times they are). But sometimes, objects are *far* less chic than they appear. Don't get me wrong, I've had some incredible experiences—like a safari in Botswana and a chateau in Saint-Tropez—but some work trips need a little more... curation...than others.

So what's a good example of a moment when my life needed a little extra zhuzhing? A trip I took to the British Virgin Islands in the winter of 2015. Those who followed me at the time saw nothing but white sand and (sunless) tanned limbs. But IRL, the trip was a disaster.

I was invited to the BVIs by a men's swimwear brand called Onia. They were about to launch their first line for women and were planning a splashy (no pun intended) influencer trip to an-nounce the collection. A friend of a friend named Brad ran the company's PR and asked if I wanted to attend.

"They've rented this amazing luxury catamaran," he gushed on the phone. "All *you* have to do is post pictures of yourself look-ing banging in their new swimsuits—which shouldn't be hard, you sexy little thing. It's a no-fucking-brainer."

Needless to say, Brad had a big personality. But his pitch was also convincing. The promise of four days in the tropics with the wind on my face and crystal-blue water sounded pretty appealing, especially considering it was winter in Manhattan. (Plus, I love an opportunity to network with my fellow influencer peers in settings less formal than fashion shows.)

At the time, I had about one million followers—which was enough to secure a free spot on the trip for me and a plus one. I almost always get paid, as well, but for this trip was just happy with a free luxury vacation. (For the sake of transparency, I now make more than $10,000 for a post. Tack on travel, and the price goes up.) So, fine. I wouldn't make any money on the trip. But you can't beat a free Caribbean vacation, especially with what Onia was promising.

I told Moe to pack her bags.

All of the influencers met at the Miami airport a week later to fly to Tortola. Some of the girls I knew and some I didn't. I remem-ber one influencer complaining that Onia hadn't sprung for first class airfare. Hell, they didn't even pay for extra legroom.

"Maybe they spent all of their budget on the boat?" I replied, eager to get out in the sun.

My optimism immediately dimmed when I saw the "luxury catamaran" on which we were to spend the next four evenings.

I'm sure the boat was perfectly nice, but Onia had *massively* oversold its size and opulence. There were only four bedrooms for twelve girls, which meant there would be three girls to every room (and that Moe and I would have to share with a stranger). Oh yeah, and there were only bunk beds. It was annoying, but I could deal. I didn't spend eight years at rustic Camp Birchmont only to freak out when things got rustic.

That's when I saw the bathroom, which was conveniently located…in the corner of each bedroom. The shower was over the toilet. In fact, the only thing separating Moe and me from our randomly assigned roommate whenever we needed to…go…was a dinky, see-through curtain. Seriously, the place was worse than my first New York apartment.

The other issue? The boat lacked both Wi-Fi and a sufficient number of power outlets, which was odd, considering this was an influencer trip. How were we going to post if our phones were dead and had no service? And where was I going to plug in my flat iron? (Tropical humidity wreaks havoc on my hair.)

Thank God Moe was there. Because after two years of working together, we had developed the ability to communicate without words:

"What the fuck is this?" I asked with a glare.

"I don't know, but it's definitely not what they promised," Moe responded with the tilt of her head.

"Should we get the fuck out of here?" I replied with a lifted eyebrow.

"Definitely," Moe agreed with a nod. She turned on her Tory Burch sandals and went to find the captain.

Five minutes later, Moe and I boarded a dinghy back to shore. As soon as we made it back to land, I whipped out my phone—thank God, service!—and found the nearest hotel with vacancies. TripAdvisor called the five star Rosewood resort "the best honeymoon destination in the Caribbean." So what if the only room left was a suite, which was far outside my emergency travel budget? Desperate times called for desperate measures.

I called Brad to explain the situation. He feigned sympathy but wasn't exactly motivated to help me. Brad had done his job when he'd gotten me on the trip. (Some PR execs don't always think about long term relationships. They just want to get you to the next trip/event/party.)

We ended up having a great, if unexpectedly expensive, time. Moe and I spent a long weekend at the Rosewood, avoiding newlyweds while we knocked back tequila sunrises. And in my defense, I still fulfilled my photo commitments for Onia. I'm a professional, and the brand had paid for both of our flights. (Don't even get me started about how awkward it was to fly back with everyone else when Monday rolled around...)

A few weeks later, just after the New Year, I was invited to a birthday party at a classic NoHo hotspot called ACME. The place had opened with a bang in 2012, a Scandinavian restaurant on the first floor and a raucous club in the basement. It has old wood floors, black leather furniture, and brick walls. Even all these years later, the place is perpetually packed with rowdy recent graduates and the artsy downtown elite.

So there we were, crowding around the birthday girl as she blew out the candles on her Magnolia Bakery cake. I've never been especially into sweets, which is a blessing in my line of work, so I took this as my cue to hit the bar. I pushed my way up front—you know how I feel about lines—and ordered my usual tequila cocktail.

That's when I felt a hand on my shoulder. I whipped around to discover a well-dressed, smiling brunette man who couldn't be more than a few years older than me.

"Can I help you?" I asked, hoping this guy wasn't about to hit on me. (It was too soon after Rob—my romantic life was closed for business.)

"Are you the same Danielle Bernstein who ditched our boat trip?" he asked with a mischievous glint. "I'm Nathan. The owner of Onia."

"I see." I took a beat to regain my composure. "In that case, I've got a bone to pick with you."

"As do I," he replied.

Nathan paid for my drink, and we settled into the nearest black booth. I was ready for him to yell at me for bailing on his floating prison-parading-as-a-catamaran. Thankfully, though, all he wanted to do was pay me a compliment.

"The palm-print one-piece that you posted for us sold out almost immediately," he explained, switching into business mode. "Now there's a three-month-long waiting list. Have you ever thought about designing a line of suits?"

And that's how I became a swimsuit mogul at two o'clock in the morning. Who would have thought that the worst influencer trip of my life would lead to one of the best things that ever happened to me? To be continued…

Marry the Brands

As the influencer industry grows, so do the amounts of money that we're paid to post and tag brands. But despite the fact that it's now a multibillion dollar global business, the industry lacks clear rules. There are barely any regulations (at least ones that are enforced), or even accepted norms, dictating how influencers should disclose when something we post is sponsored. Consumers are unknowingly bombarded by unmarked advertisements every time they look at their Instagram feed.

I, for one, have always tried to be transparent. I speak candidly about my business model, often giving my followers a behind-the-scenes look at how *WeWoreWhat* operates. Just take my 2015 interview with *Harper's Bazaar* as an example. I was the first influencer to speak openly about how much money we were getting to post. I got a lot of backlash for that article, but also significant praise and exposure. (Literally the next day I hit one million followers.)

I know I've talked a lot about transparency throughout this book, but the word means so many different things depending on which aspect of my career we're discussing. I believe that followers deserve to know when influencers are being paid to post. They should have confidence that we've not only tried every product, but that we would actually buy the thing with our own money. I have spent years building that trust with my followers, trying to be up front about what's sponsored and what's organic. I haven't been perfect, but I like to think my actions have set the bar for honesty in this industry.

Some influencers accept every paid opportunity that comes their way, whether they like the product or not. (That's why there are so many posts claiming to have discovered the ultimate weight loss tea or gummies to grow your hair.) And while I empathize with the urge to chase every paycheck—especially when you're just starting out—I also know that this type of behavior has had a negative impact on how people view our industry.

Influencers need to learn when and how *to say no.*

So why hasn't this problem been fixed? Why hasn't the industry banded together to create clear guidelines? For years people have been able to get away with bad behavior, profiting off the lack of regulations. It is only increasingly savvy consumers who are forcing the industry to adapt, and sometimes the FTC. Followers are finally taking a stand and refusing to be treated like walking, breathing credit cards.

So how am I different? If a brand reaches out for me to support the launch of their new moisturizer, Moe will ask the brand for samples. I'll spend a few weeks personally trying the product and incorporating it into my routine. If I like it, then I'll engage. If I don't, I won't.

I've also veered away from one-off posting, which started to feel very similar having a one-night stand. I now look to create long term partnerships that will have a greater impact, an approach I call *marrying a brand*. I've started to sign a lot of six-month and year-long contracts that require exclusivity—that I *only* promote one particular product in that category. This forces me to think long and hard about whether I want to limit myself to that brand before making such a big commitment. My followers can trust that I would never sign such a long contract with a product I didn't like. (It's good for the brands, too, which get an inclusive package of events, stories, and posts.)

FIJI Water is a great example of a brand that I married. Our partnership came about organically, as the best often do. A good friend of mine was hosting a class at Barry's Bootcamp, which I had never tried and honestly expected to hate. (Running makes my buns hurt more than I care to admit.)

I went to support my friend, half-assed my way through class and ducked out fifteen minutes early. As I sat in the locker room contemplating the abuse I'd just endured, I was approached by a man named Stephen who looked out of place in his business casual outfit. (I, on the other hand, was wearing head-to-toe Bandier.)

Stephen was there representing the brand sponsor of said torture experiment…I mean workout class. The Wonderful Company owns labels like FIJI Water, Wonderful Pistachios, and JUSTIN Vineyards, and was working with Barry's Bootcamp at the time. As soon as Stephen explained his job, I dug into the poor guy.

"I *love* FIJI," I said, my face still dripping with sweat from the workout. "I drink it all the time. But what the hell is *up* with your lack of a sports cap? Every time I work out, I spill half the bottle." Even my harshest critics can't say I'm not up front with my feelings.

Stephen was good-natured about my verbal assault and even invited me to the company's headquarters in Los Angeles. Assuming the meeting was about a potential partnership, I immediately waved him off. "I couldn't possibly work with FIJI Water until you introduce a sports cap." A par-for-the-course Danielle response.

Yes, I was externally snarky. But I was internally thrilled. Sure, I'd promoted some of the world's biggest fashion and beauty brands. I even had car sponsors. But a water partnership? That was not something I ever thought could be an option for me.

I flew out to Los Angeles a few weeks later, where Stephen explained that we'd met at exactly the right time…because FIJI *was* launching a sports cap later that year. He asked if I would come on board for a one-year contract and essentially become the spokesperson for their new bottle. They must have really wanted me, because they were offering more money than I ever thought possible when promoting a product so far outside my wheelhouse.

FIJI's offer also stipulated that I was not allowed to drink *any* other water brand during the term of our contract. (There's that exclusivity bit we talked about.) That meant an entire year during which I could be fired for publicly sipping on Evian. (Although truthfully Evian lost me when they got rid of the baby campaign.)

I said yes. Yes. A million times, yes.

For the next year, I took FIJI everywhere I went—to meetings, to dinner, to Pilates. Every event I hosted had FIJI on hand. I re-filled the bottles constantly and even implemented a recycling system in my home office. I introduced FIJI to other partners, like Revolve, and created some major cross promotion. In 2017, Forbes named us one of the five best marketing campaigns that year. Some consider it one of the most successful influencer partnerships of all time—one that FIJI extended at the end of that year and continues to extend.

Neither FIJI nor I could have predicted this level of success. My DM inbox is perpetually flooded with photos of followers holding their own FIJI bottles. When the FIJI girl blew up at the 2019 Golden Globes, everyone demanded to know why I wasn't on the red carpet. I am completely, inextricably associated with their brand.

So why does that matter? Because it creates trust—among my followers, my advertisers, and myself. As the influencer industry evolves, I hope we'll only see more of my peers marrying brands. I don't think consumers are satisfied anymore to see us post something once or twice. It's too easy; it doesn't inspire trust. Instead, our followers want us to get into bed with a brand—to know that we have vetted the product, have skin in the game, and are personally committed. And isn't that better for everyone?

Double Down When You Find a Good Partner

It's a good thing I ran into Nathan at ACME on that cold night in 2016, because our chance encounter changed the entire course of my career. When Nathan first asked me to design a swimwear collection for Onia, my answer was no. After everything that had gone wrong with my shoe brand, I was gun-shy about that type of collaboration. Sure, I was happy to create content on a brand's behalf. But if I was going to design my own product, I wanted to own the company—like I owned Second Skin Overalls. I wanted to have control.

Nathan, however, was a completely different person than Seth. Having previously worked at New Balance and Ed Hardy, he had a reputation as an experienced fashion insider. He had cofounded Onia back in 2009 without any outside financing, and thus maintained ownership and control of the company. (In essence, he started Onia the same way I started Second Skin Overalls.) He cared about and believed enough in his work to put his money where his mouth was. Our morals were in alignment.

Still, I wasn't about to commit without doing my own research. I asked everyone in my circle if they had ever worked with Nathan. (He got nothing but rave reviews.) and I grilled my bestie Joey who had known Nathan for years and was the one who introduced us.

Onia is vertically integrated, which means they manage their entire production process from soup to nuts. Rather than outsourcing design, manufacturing, or sales, Nathan and his cofounder had kept everything under one single roof. This meant that I could have the kind of quality control I had lacked in my previous shoe partnership.

What really sold me, though, was Onia's small size. Sure, the brand was well known. They had just produced a private label line for Barney's. But they weren't a household name. They were interested in not just my behemoth social media following, but also in my creative vision. They saw me not just as a marketing vehicle, but as a diamond-in-the-rough designer. And for someone like me, who has always seen these collaborations as a means to my own stand-alone brands, that's partnership gold.

I truly care about the products sold under my name, so much so that every contract after the Archive Shoe debacle now demands that I have one hundred percent control over everything from button selection to Pantone colors. A lot of influencers only attend a single design meeting before cashing their collaboration's check, but I like to be as involved as possible. And it shows in the finished product.

My design process is as follows. First, I reference the dozen or so folders on my phone in which I save inspiration images, usually vintage photos or old editorials. Next, I sketch the designs to the best of my untrained ability. Then I take those drawings to the technical designers at Onia who create CADs to show me style options.

I sift through hundreds of textiles to get the ideas flowing, then work with an in-house artist to create original artwork for our prints. I also attend every fitting, art direct every photo shoot (location scouting, modeling, editing), and go to the Onia offices multiple times per week. Sure, it sucks that they're located in midtown. But at least it's across from one of my favorite places to shoot content: the public library on Fifth Avenue.

I also demand to be involved when it comes to pricing. I get a lot of clothes for free, but I'm no stranger to overpaying. And now that I'm so fluent in production, I know just how little it actually costs brands to manufacture. (More often than not, we're paying for the label.) I want to make money, but also need to feel confident that I'm asking my customers to pay fair prices—that a full suit from our brand only costs $200 *because* the quality demands it, not because I demand it.

Onia's and my first line was an Intermix exclusive that sold out immediately, with just over $400,000 in sales. The next sold direct-to-consumers on Onia's website, moving $1 million worth of product in the first twenty-four hours. Our third and most recent collection sold more than $2.5 million on the day it launched in April 2019.

There are a lot of reasons why we've seen such great success. For one, I like to include my followers in the design process. I have always felt like customers are more likely to buy when they feel invested in the creation of a product. (Hell, Kickstarter has made an entire business off this concept.) I post just enough content that I don't overexpose unreleased products, which can cause copycats or, worse, kill the buzz.

As with SSO, I also listen to customer feedback. Social media provides a direct line to the girls buying my products. If you send me a direct message about my swimsuits, you get *me*. And I can also ask them questions. I'm constantly tweaking my future plans and designs based on feedback from Instagram. (The third collection was focused on more butt and boob coverage because my followers answered an Instagram Story poll when I asked.)

After three successful lines of swim, Nathan asked if I would consider designing other categories with Onia—sunglasses, ready-to-wear, whatever I wanted. At first, I said no and maintained my free agent status. But when I realized how much of my time it was taking to run SSO solo, I agreed to bring the brand under Onia's umbrella.

In August 2019, I signed a multiyear licensing deal that makes Onia my business partner for all WeWoreWhat brands—swim, overalls, and any other category that I choose to pursue. I was even given my own showroom in Onia's headquarters, a dedicated staff, and the support of a company that knows production inside out.

Of course, no relationship is perfect. After running SSO on my own for so long, I still struggle to follow Onia's strict production calendar. Nathan, for his part, doesn't always agree with how I style my showroom. (He wants matte black hangers; I prefer gold.) We fight like brother and sister, down to what snacks to stock in the office.

But for whatever intangible reason, our partnership just works. And as long as it continues to go well, I will continue to double down on working with Onia.

We've already conquered swim and overalls. Next up? Denim. Having Onia on my team has given me the time to concentrate on the areas that are important to me. As always, I remain focused on quality and fit above all else—something I credit for our unusually low return rate. My goal is for Shop WeWoreWhat to become the type of brand where customers feel comfortable buying every new SKU, confident it'll be up to standard.

It's a lofty goal—one so lofty, in fact, that I know I won't achieve it alone, without Onia.

Be More Than an Influencer

I'm often asked about the longevity of my career as an influencer. People ask, "Isn't an influencer basically a model? Will people stop paying attention when you get old? If Instagram shuts down, isn't your career over?" And while I reject the idea that my followers will abandon *We Wore What* the second I have gray hair and/or a baby bump, I understand the thought process.

The influencer industry is still so new. There's no historical evidence to show how long or how well we will perform. And while I understand why people compare us to models, I am *not* a model; I wasn't scouted at the local mall. (And we all know I spent enough of my teenage years shopping. If I were going to be discovered, it would have happened.) Models represent an untouchable ideal, whereas influencers are just real people with better lighting.

I've always tried to brand myself as this perfect mix of relatable and aspirational. That's why I'm hoping my followers will grow with me, and I think they already have. I actually look forward to sharing what it's like to get pregnant, to investigate which maternity jeans are the chicest, to adjust my content to my age.

The truth probably lies somewhere in the middle. Posting photos of myself to social media—whether it's Instagram or some new platform—will remain part of my business. But will it always represent the lion's share? Probably not.

That's why I've spent the past year figuring out how to apply my expertise and use my platform for other types of business. I've started to spend a lot of my time advising and investing in startups. I've always been business savvy and more focused on the back end of running a company. In exchange for my efforts, even if I financially invest, too, I ask for what we call "sweat equity"—part ownership of the company.

Here's an example: I struggle with situational anxiety. It's always been difficult for me to relax and fall asleep at night. So when Moe introduced me to CBD—a compound found in cannabis—I was open to seeing whether it could help with these issues.

Moe directed me to Highline Wellness, a direct-to-consumer, millennial-run CBD brand. (Basically, they are to CBD what Warby Parker is to glasses.) After using their product, I immediately noticed a huge reduction in my anxiety. I was less reactive, slept better, and was all around more "chill." This journey was shared with my followers—organically—in a series of unsponsored posts.

Chris, the CEO of Highline Wellness, reached out after seeing a huge surge in sales. He wanted to know if I would consider working together, which, of course, I would. We signed a six-month contract for me to promote the brand as an influencer.

I did all the usual things. I hosted events, posted pictures, and tagged the company in Instagram stories. By now, this was all old hat for me. But then, two months into the partnership, I had a stroke of brilliance.

I loved the product and knew the CBD category was exploding. I was also confident that I could help Highline Wellness with strategic introductions, social media strategy, and a very necessary rebranding. Their business model was there; their financials were great. They just needed that *WeWoreWhat* touch.

A few days later, I called Chris and asked to terminate our existing contract. (Naturally, this sparked some panic.) But I wasn't quitting. I merely proposed that I keep posting, but also become involved with the business. I wanted to be a strategic adviser who could help Highline Wellness rebrand and grow.

I didn't, however, want to be paid in cash for my efforts. I wanted equity in the company—2 percent—and a seat on the board. If things go well, there will be a much larger upside. And if they don't...well, I could get nothing. It's a risk I'm willing to take because I *believe* so much in the product.

So, no. I'm not running around, preparing my go-bag for the day when influencers stop being relevant. But I *am* thinking about how I can grow and diversify as a businesswoman. The type of partnership that I have with Highline Wellness is becoming increasingly common for *We Wore What*—an even more intense version of marrying a brand. I will continue to find companies that I believe in, then help them grow. I'm not just an influencer—I'm a businesswoman with more to offer than a pretty photo.

Remember Where You Came From

It was a cold morning in April 2019—the kind of day when your apartment floor is as cold as a glacier. I awoke to a series of missed calls from my agent, Jen, who lives in Los Angeles and is therefore three hours behind me. My heart started racing. *What could be so important that Jen had called so many times, so early?* I reached out right away.

"Danielle," Jen answered on the first ring. "Do you remember all those stories you told me about growing up shopping at Macy's on Long Island?"

I did. I also recalled a number of FIT afternoons spent at the Midtown Macy's, a young student on the hunt for fashion gold.

"Well, Macy's wants to partner with you!" Jen's voice was so excited that it bordered on screaming.

My heart immediately jumped for joy, but suddenly I couldn't match my agent's enthusiasm. Obviously, Macy's is a whale. They're a huge, amazing partner that offers market ubiquity to anyone who works with them. But was a department store with red tag sale items really the best fit for my brand?

Sensing my hesitation, Jen jumped into the offer. "They want you to design a single collection of ready-to-wear items under $100 for spring 2020."

The financials? A low six-figure dollar amount as an up-front against sales, which meant I would receive the cash right away and then a percentage of sales after Macy's had recouped the initial investment.

It was a really good offer. Definitely on the higher end of what I've come to expect from similar collaborations. (Most brands don't even offer up-front payment to influencers, usually just presenting a percent of sales as compensation.) It showed that they really wanted me and believed that I could sell. I told Jen I would think about it and get back to her by Macy's deadline at the end of the week.

It was definitely an interesting proposal. Just thinking about Macy's brought about a wave of nostalgia, remembering days spent wandering their Manhasset location. Partnering with the store could be a powerful nod to my Long Island self—to the girl I was before *We Wore What*, before I had my own place in the West Village, before I was sitting front row at the Saint Laurent show in

Paris. Sometimes it's easy to forget that teenager in the Sugar Lips tank top was actually me.

My current products also tend to be expensive, with a single Shop WeWoreWhat swimsuit running about $200. I wouldn't want to cheapen my existing brands *or* sacrifice the quality that my customers have come to expect by designing at a much lower price point.

My followers, however, might welcome the change. For years, they've been begging for more affordable designs. Perhaps this was an opportunity to thank my followers and show them that I'm listening—to really lean into the attainable part of my brand. Plus, Macy's could also introduce me to a new demographic that might never hear about me otherwise and bring my style to the masses.

I called Jen back with a list of questions.

Would a Macy's partnership impact my ability to partner with high-end brands? Would it affect the sales of my existing, more expensive products? Will Chanel ever invite me to their show if I have a department store line? How can I maintain quality, which everyone knows is so important to me, at a low price point?

After a lengthy conversation, I decided to turn down the offer…but with a caveat.

"If I were to work with Macy's," I told Jen, "then it would need to be a much larger partnership. You know I like to marry brands. Well, this one's gonna need a hefty prenup. A bigger up-front commitment—not just in terms of financials, but also my ongoing involvement."

I wasn't that worried about countering. If Macy's denied my request, then it wasn't meant to be. And if they came back, then Jen and I would be able to craft the perfect partnership. My dad always taught me *never* to accept someone's first offer. There is always room to negotiate, even if you're David and they're Goliath.

Two days later, Macy's returned with a new proposal: more money and a two-season commitment. I made a ballsy move and told Jen to counter—again—suggesting a one-year partnership of four ready-to-wear collections. One for each season. I would also need final approval over every step of the production process to ensure the quality didn't suffer, *and* control over everything from floor placement to name usage to when and for how much the items went on sale.

This time I was worried. I was getting *really* excited about this partnership. If Macy's walked away at this point, which they totally could…was I prepared to lose the deal?

I spent the next few days in a panic, waiting for Jen to call. When we hadn't heard from Macy's by their Friday afternoon deadline, I assumed I'd asked for too much and had turned them off to our partnership.

But then, on Monday, they came back. The new offer had a high six-figure guarantee, just shy of seven, which would make it the biggest deal I have ever struck. I also got the longer-term commitment. All this because I stuck to my guns and was a smart negotiator. Because I presented to Macy's the importance of marrying a brand and how it had worked in my previous partnerships.

I accepted, called my mom, and took the entire *WeWoreWhat* team for dinner at Il Cantinori. (Their Milanese is a better celebration than any champagne vintage.)

I'm still in the early stages of designing that first collection. The details have to remain top secret until its release in Spring 2020, right before this book comes out. Here's what I can say: I'm beyond excited to introduce a line of affordable, ready-to-wear clothing—everything from dresses to suits to blouses. The collection will also have plus sizes, a category I've yet to tackle. I can't wait to see beautiful women of all shapes and sizes wearing my designs. This partnership is so meaningful to me and I'm hoping my followers will see that.

With such a large partnership in the pipeline—and considering how much work it will take—it finally felt like the right time to grow my team. I recently hired a new assistant named Kimberlin. And since I like to promote from within, I've elevated my former assistant, Claudia, to brand coordinator. Claudia comes from a production background and is now helping to oversee all WeWoreWhat brands *and* the Macy's line. She leads everything from production calendars to communication with our partners.

Just don't expect to find the new Macy's line under the name *WeWoreWhat.* I've decided to call the collection "Danielle Bernstein." The name was extremely important to me, because I wanted to differentiate it from *WeWoreWhat.* Yes, I'm doing a more affordable line, but it will stand separately from WWW brands and have its own identity and customer base.

The other (and main) reason I wanted to put my own name on the brand, however, is to pay homage to my personal history—to the teenage Long Islander who spent so many days scouring the suburban store for the perfect dress to wear to the high school dance, or the perfect sweater for the homecoming game. Macy's literally was my adolescence in a nutshell.

Working with Macy's is the ultimate way to return to my roots—to the Danielle Bernstein presented in the early chapters of this book. I haven't always been the Glamazon I am (or pretend to be) today, and that's okay. Because no matter how many thousand-dollar dresses I buy from Net-a-Porter or Bergdorfs, I'll never forget where I came from and who I will always be: that teen shopping at Macy's. On Long Island.

Share Your Expertise

Looking back on the years since I founded *WeWoreWhat*, it's clear that my influencer peers and I have helped pioneer a new industry. It's humbling to think that such a small group of (mostly female) bloggers created a line of business that's now worth $12 billion annually and growing.

Influencers start their accounts for a myriad reasons, the most common of which is the desire to share   to share their life, their style, their viewpoint. I, however, have always wanted to take things a step further and share my expertise. That's why I recently launched a tech company aimed at sharing my best business practices with the influencer community at large. I have spent years branding myself as the business voice of my industry, and now it's time to put my money where my mouth is—to advise, teach, and assist others. To legitimize an industry I helped build.

Enter: MOE, the world's first project management platform for influencers.

When I first envisioned the platform in late 2018, a lot of people thought I was crazy. They questioned whether I had the bandwidth for such a large undertaking.

In typical Danielle fashion, I ignored their warnings and spent a year building it. Perhaps even more amazing, I managed to keep it a secret from my followers the entire time. (It was so difficult not to share something that was taking up most of my days.)

Cut to early 2018. I was at home drinking FIJI Water (#ad) with Moe and my best friend, Joey. A well-known male influencer, Joey was complaining about how unorganized his campaigns felt—how he desperately needed his own Moe. It had become an ongoing joke amongst my peers that "everybody needs a Moe" and that our efficient work relationship was one to envy.

At one point in the conversation I remember saying, "Enough! I wish I could just download Moe's brain into a computer to share with you!" The idea hung suspended in the air.

And that's when a three-thousand-watt light bulb went off in my brain. *Was* there a way for me to share Moe with the world?

If Macy's was my way to give back to my followers, then maybe a tech company could be my way of giving back to my community. How better to help other influencers than to turn my best asset, Moe, into a platform?

My message was (sort of) simple: over the past six years, Moe and I have set forth the best practices for how an influencer can successfully work with a brand. Now it was time to share those inner workings with my peers.

To understand MOE the platform, you need to first understand Moe the human. To understand our workflow. When a brand submits a partnership request, it goes to my powerhouse agent, Jen. She vets the proposal, then presents me with the choice projects she thinks might work.

Once I have agreed to a partnership in theory, Jen goes through the contract and pulls out what is known as the "scope of work." This is just a fancy phrase for *whatever I am actually committing to do*—for example, two Instagram stories, one blog post, and attend an event in exchange for *x* dollars. (Jen is also careful to point out any travel or exclusivity, which requires additional thought.)

Once the contract is signed, Jen sends the scope of work to Moe, who records everything in her handy-dandy notebook. (Seriously, we're talking about a day planner straight out of 1982). She plugs dates into a Google calendar and payment details into an Excel spreadsheet, but it's really Moe's analog notebook that powers the *WeWoreWhat* business.

Every week at our office starts with Moe checking that notebook for whatever is on the agenda that week. (If we ever lost that damn spiral, we'd be completely screwed.) If it sounds complicated, that's because it is. It's a convoluted process involving lots of different people (Jen, Moe, my assistants) and platforms (Excel, GCal, Moe's notebook).

What really stands out about this workflow is that it's entirely dependent on Moe. One of the most common things I hear from fellow influencers is, "How do I get my own Moe?"

The influencer industry has always been the Wild West of marketing. But now there are billions of dollars getting thrown around, and no one has created a centralized platform to help us run our businesses. There is no Salesforce or Trello for influencers. I interviewed everyone from Olivia Culpo to Girl With No Job, and no one had found a tool that worked.

So what is MOE? MOE is a tech platform created to streamline the influencer workflow. I used my own expertise and experience to create a one-of-a-kind tool that addresses an influencer's many pain points—things like scheduling and project management. I also created a feature that formalizes the invoicing process, reminds brands about delinquent payments, and helps ensure influencers get paid on time. (How many hours of my life have I spent chasing paychecks?) It's an end-to-end solution to help make influencers more efficient. More legit.

MOE finally launched at the same time I was finishing this book. I was more nervous about this product release than any other product in my life. I literally could *not* sleep for weeks before, staying up to drink warm milk with my new boyfriend and worrying whether MOE would fail.

Why was I so anxious? Because I was going to need to raise money. I personally poured almost $200,000 into MOE's development, but the company needed more. To do this right, I would need an outside investment to the tune of $1.2 million—to fund the product development, to rent an office, to make those first few hires.

Like most entrepreneurs, I chose to start with a "friends and family" round of investment. (That's money that comes from people in your existing network, as opposed to pitching complete strangers, private equity firms, etc.) Keep in mind, even though I have made millions of dollars for myself and brands, I have yet to *raise* a single dollar. This was a completely new experience.

I decided to turn to my old friend Google—because I may not have an MBA, let alone a bachelor's degree, but I do have the internet. I was able to find some great examples of pitch decks and set about building the PowerPoint I would need in order to approach investors.

The first person I pitched was my father. To set the scene, we met in the same conference room where I pitched the benefits of dropping out of FIT all those years ago. Once again, I had donned a suit for the occasion and came with my presentation ready. Not only did I convince him, but also my brothers, best friends, and even some very notable people in the fashion industry to invest.

MOE launched on October 2, 2019, and already has more signups than we could have ever expected. Sure, the numbers don't give me the same instant gratification that I'm used to with product launches. But they are *huge* for this type of tech business. I have been told on more than one occasion that this is a marathon, not a sprint. That the hard work starts now.

It's definitely going to be a hustle, but I'm confident my team and I can stay on track. We *have* to stay on track if we want to legitimize and create order in this industry. In the short time that MOE has been live, it's already become one of the most fulfilling ventures of my career. I can now call myself a tech founder and CEO.

Through it all, I've realized that I really do have a responsibility to support my industry. It's been so good to me. I have learned so much from my years as an influencer. But all the knowledge in the world means nothing unless you're willing to share it.

Hey Guys, It's Me

Hey, guys. Danielle here. I've been dying to talk to you this entire time, but everyone—my cowriter, my editor, my publisher—told me not to break the fourth wall. But if you didn't know before reading this book, then you definitely know now: I have never been one for following the rules…and so here I am. Talking to you. Directly. The way I do every day on @WeWoreWhat.

Hopefully you've learned something from the past two hundred pages. Maybe now you'll be able to choose the right business partner, or save yourself from dating a Red Flag Guy. It would give me indescribable pleasure to know that you have learned from not only my successes, but also my failures.

Although writing this book has been a wonderful process, it's also one of the most difficult things I've ever done—as scary as it was exciting. Telling my story has forced me to be my most vulnerable self. Which, surprise, isn't something that comes naturally to me. I'm more comfortable when wearing my (designer label) armor.

It would have been easier to keep pushing forward without writing this book. To keep growing *We Wore What* without considering the past. Without digging up my family's history. Without revisiting former loves. Without looking back on the many errors I have made in my relatively short time on this planet.

So why did I write this? I wrote it as much for me as I wrote it for you guys, just another step in my quest to become my best self. The hard work started about five years ago when yet another romantic relationship fell apart. It was then that I met my life coach, Stacy. (I know the term might sound a little woo-woo. But she changed my life.) I found Stacy because I didn't like the person I was. Sure, I was doing well in business. But I had focused so much on my career that I had forgotten about me. About self-improvement.

I was deeply unhappy. Unanchored, uneven. My weekly appointments with Stacy forced me to do the hard work of introspection, which I would have avoided if left to my own devices. If it weren't for Stacy, it would have been easy to keep plodding forward without having to confront my issues and insecurities. She taught me how to become the best version of myself.

Writing this book has allowed me to put it all out there and reveal the most authentic Danielle. I can't thank you enough for coming along for the ride.

I suppose what I'm trying to say comes down to the book's title: *This Is Not a Fashion Story*. Early readers of this manuscript kept asking what the phrase meant. "If it's about you, then it's *obviously* a fashion story. Fashion is *who you are*."

But fashion is only a small part of me. That's why I didn't write a book about how to take the perfect Instagram photo or how to find the best agent. I'm not just an influencer; I'm also a daughter, a sister, a boss, a role model, a lover, a friend. I wanted to seize this opportunity to reflect and share all these different sides of myself, which you might not otherwise see.

So where am I now? At twenty-seven years old, I have finally found a man who is both nice *and* challenges me at the same time. Our relationship is easy, healthy, and exactly as it should be. I'm really hoping he's the one.

After years of hard work with both Melissa and Stacy, I have grown and matured in ways I didn't know were possible. I'm a better leader and a better friend. A better person.

Most important, though, I learned how to be happy, how to be kinder to myself, how to be vulnerable without fear of embarrassment. I can accept that I've made mistakes and will continue to make them. Rather than be ashamed, I will share these faults with my followers. Not only will it teach you guys not to repeat my errors, but it will also give me an opportunity to improve and deepen our connection.

Please write to me and share your own tales. Because, after all, none of our stories are just fashion stories. No one is that one-sided.

They're just *our* stories—our own twisted, unique, and inspiring tales. And that's what makes us beautiful.

I hope you feel closer to me after reading my story. I hope you know that I'm more than just *WeWoreWhat*. I'm Danielle Bernstein, the Long Island girl who once dreamed of making it big in New York City. This is not a fashion story; it's just *my* story.